The

# FORTUNE FORUM
### Code

2. JULY 2015   From Avid.

# The
# FORTUNE FORUM
## Code

*For a Sustainable Future*

Vijay Mehta

VM Centre for Peace
for
Fortune Forum

First published in 2006 by
VM Centre for Peace
97 Commercial Road
London
E1 1RD
Phone 0207 377 2111          Fax 0207 377 2999
Email info@vmpeace.org
www.vmpeace.org

ISBN 0 9553914 0 7

A CIP Catalogue is available from the British Library.

Printed by Russell Press Ltd (0115 978 4505)

To all people working tirelessly towards ending global poverty, the protection of the environment, halting the onslaught of deadly diseases and peacebuilding. May your work inspire others, to join you in your noble endeavour.

# About FORTUNE FORUM

The Fortune Forum Summit event, held on 26th September 2006, in London, marked the launch of the Fortune Forum Club initiative. Former US President Bill Clinton addressed The Summit with the keynote speech. Other speakers included Michael Douglas, Deepak Chopra and Zac Goldsmith. The Fortune Forum Code is designed to encapsulate and advocated the Fortune Forum ethos.

Fortune Forum staged its first philanthropic summit to assist major humanitarian causes and campaigns worldwide, comprising; heads of the world's largest foundations, global leaders, celebrities and influential entrepreneurs as its members. The Summit was hosted as a Gala Dinner Forum, in an intimate glamorous setting, and notably, had a clear philanthropic agenda.

Fortune Forum is a not-for-profit, non-political organisation and so all proceeds from the Forum will go to charities, aid organisations and development programs. The Summit is a platform for eminent speakers and music legends to foster generosity, and to mobilise international solidarity. It will send an international message to promote a culture of giving.

The world's greatest philanthropists are today's agents of change and decisive policy-makers. The Summit will augment philanthropic power and advance the moral duty of social investment for global development. Our future resides in the creative force of the interrelated global goals which embody the message, that is, Fortune Forum.

www.fortuneforum.org

# Contents

# Fortune Forum Code

# Vijay Mehta

# Fortune Forum Code

Vijay Mehta

# Acknowledgements

I am grateful to the Fortune Forum charity board, especially its founder, Renu Mehta, for encouraging me to write the Fortune Forum Code book. This book will accompany the Fortune Forum series of high-level events, taking place in London.

The book is inspired by the themes of the Fortune Forum Summit which are reducing global poverty, environmental sustainability, halting the onslaught of deadly diseases, and education for bringing peace and harmony in the world. Some of these chapters in the book were originally part of lectures I gave at different venues around the world which can be accessed at www.vmpeace.org.

I am grateful to the United Nations and its agencies, UNDP, WHO and UNEP, and other websites from where some facts, figures and material has been accessed to highlight the problems and solutions of global poverty, environment and worldwide diseases.

At the launch of the Fortune Forum event, all of the distinguished delegates will be presented a copy of the book. It is to encourage their participation and continued support for initiatives which will help save our precious planet.

It has been great working with the team of Fortune Forum in advancing the philanthropic agenda. I would also like to thank Abdul Muhib and Carolyn Smith for the research and index of the book.

**Vijay Mehta**
London, September 2006

# Fortune Forum Code

## Glossary

| | |
|---|---|
| **AIDS** | Acquired Immune Deficiency Syndrome |
| **ASEAN** | Association of Southeast Asian Nations |
| **BWI** | Bretton Woods institutions |
| **CD** | Conference on Disarmament |
| **CFC** | Chlorofluorocarbons |
| **DFID** | Department for International Development (UK) |
| **ECOSOC** | United Nations Economic and Social Council |
| **EU** | European Union |
| **FAO** | Food and Agricultural Organization |
| **FCO** | Foreign and Commonwealth Office |
| **GA** | General Assembly |
| **GATT** | General Agreement on Tariffs and Trade |
| **GDP** | Gross Domestic Product |
| **GNP** | Gross National Product |
| **G8** | Group of Eight |
| **HDI** | Human Development Index |
| **HIPC** | Heavily indebted poor country |
| **ILO** | International Labour Organization |
| **IMF** | International Monetary Fund |
| **ITER** | International Thermonuclear Experimental Reactor |
| **LDC** | Least Developed Country |
| **MDG** | Millennium Development Goals |
| **NEPAD** | New Partnership for Africa's Development |
| **NGO** | Non-Governmental Organisation |
| **ODA** | Official Development Assistance |
| **OECD** | Organisation for Economic Cooperation and Development |
| **OSCE** | Organization for Security and Cooperation in Europe |
| **PRS** | Poverty Reduction Strategy |
| **P-5** | Permanent Five Members of the Security Council: the |

|        |                                                                    |
|--------|--------------------------------------------------------------------|
|        | US, UK, Russian Federation, France and China                       |
| **SALW**   | Small Arms and Light Weapons                                   |
| **SAP**    | Structural Adjustment Programme                                |
| **SC**     | Security Council                                               |
| **TRIPS**  | Agreement on Trade-Related Aspects of Intellectual Property Rights |
| **UN**     | United Nations                                                 |
| **UNAIDS** | Joint United Nations Programme on HIV/AIDS                     |
| **UNCTAD** | United Nations Conference on Trade and Development             |
| **UNDP**   | United Nations Development Programme                           |
| **UNEP**   | United Nations Environmental Programme                         |
| **UNECA**  | United Nations Economic Commission for Africa                  |
| **UNESCO** | United Nations Educational, Scientific and Cultural Organization |
| **UNICEF** | United Nations Children's Fund                                 |
| **WHO**    | World Health Organization                                     |
| **WMD**    | Weapons of Mass Destruction                                   |
| **WTO**    | World Trade Organization                                      |

# 1
# Introduction

*Why the implementation of the Millennium Development Goals
are crucial for international development*

## Opening opportunities for all

At the start of the twenty-first century we live in a divided world. The size of the divide poses a fundamental challenge to the global, human community. Part of that challenge is ethical and moral. As Nelson Mandela said: "Massive poverty and obscene inequality are such terrible scourges of our times - times in which the world boasts breathtaking advances in science, technology, industry and wealth accumulation - that they have to rank alongside slavery and apartheid as social evils." The twin scourges of poverty and inequality can be defeated - but progress has been faltering and uneven.

Rich countries, as well as poor, have an interest in changing this picture. Reducing the gulf in wealth and opportunity that divides the human community is not a zero-sum game in which some have to lose so that others gain. Extending opportunities for people in poor countries to lead long and healthy lives, to get their children a decent education and to escape poverty will not diminish the well-being of people in rich countries. On the contrary, it will help build shared prosperity and strengthen our collective security. In our interconnected world a future built on the foundations of mass poverty in the midst of plenty is economically inefficient, politically unsustainable and morally indefensible.

Debates about trends in global income distribution continue to rage.

# Vijay Mehta

Less open to debate is the sheer scale of inequality. The world's richest 500 individuals have a combined income greater than that of the poorest 416 million. Beyond these extremes, the 2.5 billion people living on less than $2 a day - 40% of the world's population - account for 5% of global income. The richest 10%, almost all of whom live in high-income countries, account for 54%.

An obvious corollary of extreme global inequality is that even modest shifts in distribution from top to bottom could have dramatic effects on poverty. Using a global income distribution database, we estimate a cost of $300 billion for lifting 1 billion people living on less than $1 a day above the extreme poverty line threshold. That amount represents 1.6% of the income of the richest 10% of the world's population. Of course, this figure describes a static transfer. Achieving sustainable poverty reduction requires dynamic processes through which poor countries and poor people can work their way out of extreme deprivation.

But in our highly unequal world, greater equity would provide a powerful catalyst for poverty reduction and progress towards the Millennium Development Goals (MDGs).[1] These important goals were agreed at the Millennium Summit in New York in September 2000. These provide a new compact for international cooperation to free our fellow men, women and children from the abject and dehumanising conditions of extreme poverty to which more than a billion of them are now subjected.

---

[1] 1. Eradicate extreme poverty and hunger by half, 2. Achieve universal primary education, 3. Promote gender equality and empower women, 4. Reduce child mortality, 5. Improve maternal health, 6. Combat HIV/AIDS, malaria and other diseases, 7. Ensure environmental sustainability, and 8. Develop a global partnership for development.

# Fortune Forum Code

## Poverty and the state of our cities

In the cities world over, residents of slums, while only 6% of the city population of the developed countries, constitute a staggering 78.2% of urbanites in the least-developed countries"; and China added more city-dwellers in the 1980s than did of all Europe (including Russia) in the entire 19th century. For the first time the urban population of the earth will outnumber the rural; there will soon be more people living in cities than in the country.

But vast "peri-urban" developments, horizontal spreads of unplanned squats and shantytowns, unsightly dumps of humans and waste, where child labour is the norm, child prostitution is commonplace, gangs and paramilitaries rule and there is no access to clean water or sanitation, let alone to education or democratic institutions.

As is evident from Beirut's Quarantina, to Santa Cruz Meyehualco in Mexico City, to Russia's ex-socialist company towns, to Rio de Janeiro's favelas, and to Cairo's City of the Dead, where one million people use Mameluke tombs as prefabricated housing components. It is estimated that there are already some 200,000 such slums worldwide. The slum is becoming the blueprint for cities of the future, which, rather than being made out of glass and steel as envisioned by earlier generations of urbanists, are instead largely constructed out of crude brick, straw, recycled plastic, cement blocks and scrap wood.[2] The majority of the world's population living in slums is poor, oppressed, dispossessed and starving. Generating conditions for raising their living standards will be a global challenge facing us this century.

---

[2] I. Sansom, "Shantytown Apocalypse," The Guardian, 19 August 2006

# Vijay Mehta

## One goal, two agendas

Let us examine on a global level what are the complex present-day threats and challenges, risks and responsibilities? How are they different and what is the changing nature of reality? We will further see if the old institutions are fit to deal with the new threats. If not, can they be reformed or do we need new institutions to replace them? How effective we are in dealing with the present challenges will depend on what type of legacy we will leave behind for future generations.

Looking at the world horizon today, we see two distinct agendas followed by the countries of the North and the South (developing world). The countries in the North are relentlessly pursuing the war on terror and things are viewed from the angle of the threat of war and terrorism. It also includes paranoia of countries developing nuclear weapons anywhere in the world and a confrontational policy to stop them.

In contrast, the countries in the South are battling with hunger, disease and crippling poverty. The most important goal for them is freedom from want and fear, for which their prime objective is acceleration of development and the implementation of the MDGs.

The world at present is blindingly pursuing these two agendas – like two ships silently passing each other by, in the dead of night, not talking to each other, and to the detriment of each other.

Kofi Annan, recently addressed the dilemma as such:

> "First, we are all in the same boat. More than ever before, the human race faces global problems - from poverty and inequality to nuclear proliferation, from climate change to bird flu, from terrorism to HIV/AIDS, from ethnic cleansing

and genocide to trafficking in the lives and bodies of human beings. So it obviously makes sense to come together and work out global solutions.

And secondly, the three freedoms which all human beings crave - freedom from want, freedom from war or large-scale violence, and freedom from arbitrary or degrading treatment - are closely interconnected. There is no long-term security without development. There is no development without security. And no society can long remain secure, or prosperous, without respect for human rights and the rule of law."[3]

The scale of the challenge facing the world at the start of the 10-year countdown to 2015 is daunting as to how the MDGs can be implemented. Its focus is on what governments in rich countries can do to keep their side of the global partnership bargain. This does not imply that governments in developing countries have no responsibility. On the contrary, they have primary responsibility. No amount of international cooperation can compensate for the actions of governments that fail to prioritise human development, to respect human rights, to tackle inequality, or to root out corruption. But without a renewed commitment to cooperation backed by practical action, the MDGs will be missed and the Millennium Declaration will go down in history as just one more empty promise.

Universal primary education and getting rid of illiteracy is one of the eight Millennium Development Goals, to be achieved by 2015. However, the reality is that one in six adults on the planet cannot read or write. Some 600 million women and 300 million men remain illiterate around the world.

---

[3] Kofi Annan, 'Statesmanship, confidence-rebuilding required for UN capable of coping with today's crises,' UNA-UK Association (London), 31 January 2006.

# Vijay Mehta

The biggest hindrance to education and development is military spending and war-related costs. The US government spends approximately $1 million every minute on military expenditure. The recent increased military spending once again for the sixth successive year rose to the trillion dollar mark since the height of the Cold War, an average of $162 per person, with the United States accounting for nearly half - 47 per cent - of the total at $455 billion and the UK at $47 billion.[4]

## Sustainable development: a global challenge

Eradicating poverty is the greatest global challenge facing the world today and an indispensable requirement for sustainable development, particularly for developing countries." This quote is taken from the Plan of Implementation of the Johannesburg World Summit on Sustainable Development in 2002 and it reflects a perception of sustainable development that most people share. The concept must be understood in terms of human needs, rights and responsibility towards the environment as well as in terms of solidarity – between generations and between communities. Unless we keep this in mind too many people will persist in maintaining that we should deal with poverty and growth first and then take a look at the environment.[5]

When Wangari Maathai was awarded the Nobel Peace Prize, it was a timely reminder that we must take a holistic approach to environmental management, human rights, poverty reduction and peace. This sounds simple, but in practice our thinking and actions tend to be compartmentalised, focusing on one or other of these

---

[4] Stockholm International Peace Research Institute, "Recent Trends in Military Expenditure," SIPRI Military Expenditure and Arms Production Project. Available at http://www.sipri.org/content/milap/milex/mex_trends.html

[5] The Environment and Poverty Times (Sep 2006) "Sustainable development : a global challenge," A publication by UNEP/GRID-Arendal

goals. In all our efforts to implement the MDGs it is essential to remember that sustainable development and its three pillars – economic, social and environmental development – are implicit in all the goals. Achieving MDG number 7 on environmental sustainability is vital to reaching the other MDGs on poverty, health and gender equality.

The MDGs and the decisions taken at the Johannesburg summit have contributed effectively to focusing the world agenda on the challenges associated with all three pillars. There was a time when it was difficult to convince world leaders and politicians to focus on poverty and environmental issues. Fortunately this is no longer the case. To mention but one example: Africa and climate change were at the top of the agenda at the Gleneagles G8 meeting in 2005.

Climate change is a reminder of the fact that poor people are most likely to be the first victims and the greatest sufferers of environmental degradation. The poor are more vulnerable than others to environmental hazards and environment-related conflicts and least able to cope with them when they occur. They also tend to be most dependent on the environment and direct use of natural resources, and are therefore most severely affected by environmental degradation and lack of access to natural resources.

The 2005 Millennium Summit was a unique opportunity to reaffirm the global partnership for achieving the goals and the principle that every country must take the primary responsibility for its own economic and social development. But the summit failed to live up to expectations and largely did not achieve the targets it had set to reach.

The UN report on the status of MDG implementation answers some of these questions, noting in particular that unprecedented gains against poverty have been achieved since 1990. The number of people living in extreme poverty has fallen by 130 million. This progress has taken place against the backdrop of overall population growth of more than 800 million people in the developing regions.

But 1.2 billion people are still living on less than $1 a day and half the developing world lacks access to sanitation. Every week in the developing world 200,000 children under 5 die of disease and 10,000 women die giving birth. In addition, we need to adjust ourselves to the new geography of poverty. Some regions score highly on most of the goals, whereas sub-Saharan Africa is lagging behind. In a few years' time, for the first time in history, there will be more people, in absolute figures, living in extreme poverty in Africa than in Asia.

The report of the UN Millennium Project states quite clearly that most of the world is failing to reduce the loss of biodiversity. All developing regions have experienced substantial environmental degradation over the past decade, which could very well worsen as a result of long-term, man-made global climate change. Many countries are struggling because their natural resource base – specifically the forests, fisheries, soil and water – is being progressively degraded and polluted.

In March 2005, the UN Millennium Ecosystem Assessment, Living beyond our Means[6], confirmed these negative trends. In particular, it focused on ecosystem services and their benefits for people, concluding with a stark warning: human activity is putting such a strain on the planet's ecosystems that we can no longer take for granted their ability to sustain future generations.

We should take very seriously the report's insistence that our planet's natural assets must be seen as part of the fight against poverty. Many of the regions facing the greatest challenges achieving the goals must

---

[6] See http://www.maweb.org

also cope with severe ecosystem degradation. The report clearly states that, "development policies aimed at reducing poverty that ignore the impact of our current behaviour on the natural environment may well be doomed to failure."

The conclusion I draw from these two reports is that we need to focus more on Africa and the environment. The MDGs can and must be met. But they will not be met unless we all, donors and developing countries alike, improve on our past performance. We need to do more, and to do it better and faster.

## Promoting global reform agenda

If we are to reach the MDGs, we need to promote our global reform agenda on four main fronts. First, we need to reform international framework conditions. Trade and market access, investment and debt must be addressed, and we must all be willing to help establish a level playing field.

Second we need donor reform, with more and better aid. The Paris Declaration on aid effectiveness, with its commitments, timetables and targets, is now the benchmark for gauging the shift from the uncoordinated donor circus of the past to the country-owned, country-led development of the future. This is why the Paris Declaration must be endorsed. What makes it different from previous agreements is that fact that 12 indicators to monitor progress in achieving results and it creates stronger mechanism for accountability.[7]

Third we need governance reform in developing countries. Development starts from the inside. Lasting development in any

---

[7] The Paris Declaration, endorsed on 2 March 2005, is an international agreement on aid effectiveness.

country requires responsible and transparent governance, including a strong and persistent focus on efforts to combat corruption. This goes for environmental policies as well. And fourth we need to mobilise the private sector and civil society. One creates jobs and promotes economic growth, and the other seeks to empower the poor. Both are essential for fighting poverty.

If we lack the will to reform the way we work, the goals will end up being little more than wishful thinking. They will join all the other well-intentioned initiatives in the graveyard of broken promises to the poor, and our generation will have failed its most important test. We cannot let this happen.

Agreement on the MDGs and the Johannesburg principles was an outstanding achievement on the part of the UN. But it will only be a true victory when the goals are reached. Only when deadlines are kept, targets are met and the poor see improvements in their own lives which do not jeopardise sustainable use of resources, only then, shall we all have succeeded. Secretary-General Kofi Annan said: "All our efforts will be in vain if their results are reversed by continued degradation of the environment and depletion of our natural resources." We must ensure that the efforts of the international community reflect this view of sustainable development. Let us renew and strengthen our resolve and make sure we deliver the results on time by 2015.

We should place emphasis on environment and sustainable development; on gender issues and the shaping of a coordinated response to globalisation, to terrorism and other global challenges like HIV/AIDS. This should be done while engaged in the prevention of conflict and, where conflict has broken out, in peacekeeping, peacemaking and peace building.

The renovation needs to take place simultaneously on each pillar of international cooperation. Failure in any one area will undermine the foundations for future progress. More effective rules in international trade will count for little in countries where violent conflict blocks opportunities to participate in trade. Increased aid without fairer trade rules will deliver suboptimal results. And peace without the prospects for improved human welfare and poverty reduction that can be provided through aid and trade will remain fragile.

This book deals with the themes of global poverty, environmental sustainability and worldwide diseases which the Fortune Forum identifies. There is a specific chapter dealing with Africa, and the exceptional challenges it faces. The chapter on education deals with conflicts and violence which is too often a barrier to development. It outlines the need to nurture a culture of peace which is a set of values, attitudes and way of life based on principles of freedom, equality and justice.

One of the central messages of the book is to understand the interlinking global agendas of development, security and environment. These issues need to be dealt with collectively as an overarching agenda for the progress of the world. In particular, the section 'the world in 2006 and beyond' looks at the state of the world today and tomorrow, and makes observations as to how we see our future in completing these pressing issues. The chapter, Ways for a better world, is a collection of quotes and ideas for action and inspiration.

The appendices to the book are an important addition to the main chapters. They include the preamble to the United Nations Charter. The Universal Declaration of Human Rights includes its preamble and relevant articles to poverty and human rights. The eight UN Millennium Development Goals are a reminder of what we have to achieve by 2015. "Investing in Development" is a significant report which outlines why the goals are important and why we are falling thus far.

The insertion of the WHO Constitution in the appendices is to remind us that health of people is not simply the absence of disease or infirmity but a state of complete physical, mental and social well-being. There is also a brief summary of the Kyoto Protocol, which is the benchmark for environmental protection. The declaration and programme on the UNESCO Culture of Peace is to reaffirm the fact that without peace education, the other areas of development are not sustainable.

The book contains invaluable contributions from other sources. In particular, the United Nations and its agencies (UNDP, WHO, UNEP) where some facts, figures and materials have been accessed.

The destination of the book is action-orientated. What we need is political will, action and more innovative breakthrough in solutions for a sustainable future.

# 2
# Global Poverty

*Can the widening gap between the rich and poor be reduced?*

## Introduction[8]

At the dawn of the new century, the issue of development - how to create it and sustain it - undoubtedly remains one of the most daunting challenges facing the international community. In recognition of the need to find solutions for eradicating global poverty and hunger, along with creating more effective ways for distributing aid in developing countries, the United Nations adopted the Millennium Development Goals (MDGs) in 2000. To some, this may have appeared to be only a very ambitious agenda, but for others it is more than just an acknowledgment that something must be done. It really is about devising a strategy, a plan of action, that promises the poor such essentials as primary education, basic health, and a reversal of AIDS by 2015. It is also about taking the steps needed to ensure that these promises will be turned into concrete action.[9]

The continent hardest hit by poverty is Africa. Sub-Saharan Africa has the highest rates of overall and infant mortality on the planet, the shortest life expectancy (average life expectancy has declined from 50 to 46 since 1990), the lowest per capita income, and the fastest

---

[8] This is part of a discussion paper by Vijay Mehta – "Development in Africa: shaking the curse of poverty, hunger and disease," 2 July 2005, Edinburgh, Scotland. **www.vmpeace.org**

[9] See transcripts of remarks of Fairer Globalisation Series, "Development agenda 2006: from ideas into action," Carnegie Council, 1 December 2005. http://www.carnegiecouncil.org

rate of population increase. Whereas in the developed world less than one in 100 children die before the age of five, in most of sub-Saharan Africa that number is one in 10, and in 14 countries it is one in five. In sub-Saharan Africa, the number of people living on less than $1 a day has increased since 1990. While under nourishment decreased worldwide in the 1990s, it increased in Africa.

More than 1 billion people still live below the extreme poverty line of $1 a day, and 30,000 die from poverty each day. More than 3 billion - more than half of humanity - live in poverty, with less than $2 per day. Over 1 billion people have no access to health care. Out of the population of the developing countries, 66% have no toilets, nor even latrines.

In the developing world, 866 million people are illiterate. Two billion have no link to an electricity network. Some 80% of the world's population has no access to basic forms of telecommunications. There are more telephone lines in Manhattan, New York than in whole of sub-Saharan Africa and half the human race have never used the telephone.

Large portion of the world's population living in absolute poverty are under the age of 15 years old, out of which 70% are women and girls. A World Bank study estimated that it would take 70 years to double the daily income of every African living on $1 dollar a day. Will it really take more than three generations to enable every African to earn the paltry sum of $2 dollars a day?

Some of the causes of poverty are unserviceable debt, under-investment in science and technology, unjust trade rules, the onslaught of diseases, ethnic conflicts, corruption, high level of unemployment, and the lack of infrastructure and education. The world is in for a rough ride if we remain complacent.

# Fortune Forum Code

Eleven million children die every year – 30,000 per day from preventable and treatable causes. More than half a million women die each year during pregnancy or childbirth. Malaria and TB kills as many each years as AIDS, and represent a severe drain on national economies.

In Congo, 4 million people have died in the civil war which the West barely noticed. The country once plundered for rubber is now pillaged for diamonds, copper, cobalt, zinc and gold.

Since 1990, while developing countries' per capita income has increased an average of 3 per cent annually, the number of people living in extreme poverty has increased in some regions by more than 100 million people. In at least 54 countries, average per capita income has declined over the same period. Every year, almost 11 million children die from preventable diseases and more than half a million women die during pregnancy or childbirth. Increasing poverty is accompanied by an increase in global inequality and income inequality in many poor countries. In parts of Latin America, for example, the income of the wealthiest fifth of households is 30 times greater than that of the poorest fifth. Worldwide, women and youth are disproportionately poor.

When poverty is added to ethnic or regional inequalities, the grievances that stoke civil violence are compounded. While it may not reach the level of war, the combination of a surging youth population, poverty, urbanisation and unemployment has resulted in increased gang violence in many cities of the developing world. We should not allow our greatest asset, the youth, to become a threat to our security.

Current trends indicate persistent and possibly worsening food insecurity in many countries, especially in sub-Saharan Africa. Population growth in the developing world and increased per capita consumption in the industrialised world have led to greater demand for scarce resources. The loss of arable land, water scarcity, overfishing, deforestation and the alteration of ecosystems pose daunting challenges for sustainable development. The world's population is expected to increase from 6.3 billion today to 8.9 billion in 2050, with nearly all of that growth occurring in the countries least equipped to absorb it. Feeding such a rapidly growing population will only be possible if agricultural yields can be increased significantly and sustainably.

With the adoption of the MDGs in 2000, the international community committed itself to dramatically reduce poverty by 2015. Assessments by the Millennium Project indicate that, while some regions of the world are on track to reduce by half the proportion of people living on less than $1 a day, other regions have regressed.

In the area of reducing child mortality and increasing primary education enrolment, the world continues to lag behind its commitments. Little has been done to address the gender aspects of the goals. Although rich and poor countries have pledged to take action to address social and economic threats, pledges have not materialised into resources and action and long -term commitments are scant. All states need to recommit themselves to the goals of eradicating poverty, achieving sustained economic growth and promoting sustainable development.

The MDGs should be placed at the centre of national and international poverty -reduction strategies. The dramatic shortfall in resources required to meet the goals must be redressed, and the commitments to sound policies and good governance at all levels must be fulfilled. For the least developed countries, official development assistance (ODA) will be crucial and should be structured to support countries' goals-based poverty reduction strategies.

# Fortune Forum Code

The many donor countries which currently fall short of the United Nations 0.7 per cent gross national product (GNP) target for ODA should establish a timetable for reaching it. Innovative approaches like the International Finance Facility should be encouraged to finance development.

In Monterrey and Johannesburg, leaders agreed that poverty alleviation is undermined by continuing inequities in the global trading system. Seventy per cent of the world's poor live in rural areas and earn their income from agriculture. They pay a devastating cost when developed countries impose trade barriers on agricultural imports and subsidise agricultural exports. In 2001, the World Trade Organization (WTO) Doha Declaration explicitly committed signatories to put the needs and interests of developing countries at the heart of negotiations over a new trade round.

Governance reforms and improvements in trading opportunities will not by themselves bring about meaningful poverty alleviation in a significant number of the least developed countries - many of them in sub-Saharan Africa – where development efforts are undermined by poor infrastructure, low productivity agriculture, endemic disease and crippling levels of external debt. Developed countries will also have to do more to address the challenge in the poorest countries of debt sustainability – which should be redefined as the level of debt consistent with achieving the goals. Lender governments and the international financial institutions should provide highly indebted poor countries with greater debt relief, longer rescheduling and improved access to global markets.

# Vijay Mehta

## Globalisation and the widening wealth gap

It is not simply the gulf between the wealthiest and poorest nations that is expanding. Within nations, too, there is an ever-growing divide between those who have benefited from economic growth, and those whom it has bypassed. There are growing inequalities within countries, between the richest and the poorest.

There is some mobility within middle-income countries, especially in South-East Asia, where a country like Taiwan has actually experienced a fall in inequality.

In general, however, the increase in globalisation has not contributed to a closing of the rich-poor gap. Brazil, for instance, has one of worst income distributions in the world. Globalisation (liberalisation) should have been a force for good, and an economic model based on unimpeded flow of capital, goods, and labour between countries.

However, the economic and social prosperity it brings, enhanced the wealth and capital of the developed world. It violates the human rights of developing societies, claims to bring prosperity, yet often simply amounts to plundering and profiteering. Negative effects include cultural assimilation via cultural imperialism, the export of artificial wants, and the destruction or inhibition of authentic local and global community, ecology and cultures.

## Global arms trade, conflict and poverty

In 2005, there are 249 political conflicts. Two of them are wars and 22 are severe crises, making a total of 24 conflicts being carried out with a massive amount of violence. 74 conflicts are classified, as crises, meaning violence is used only occasionally. In contrast, there are 151 non-violent conflicts, which can be differentiated in 86 manifest and 65 dormant conflicts.[10]

- A typical civil war in a developing country costs, on average, US$54 billion. This includes the loss of human lives, increased military spending, destruction of infrastructure, and the reduction of economic growth in the region.

- Some 300,000 children serve as child soldiers across the world. In the past decade six million children have been injured by armed conflict, and two million have been killed.

- Of the 150 wars fought between the end of World War II and the mid-1990s, more than 90 per cent occurred in the developing world.

- Over half of all current civil wars are due to the collapse of a peace process. In the first five years following a conflict, the risk of reversion to war is about 39 per cent.

The sheer scale of destruction that intense conflict brings – particularly in the developing world – demands engagement from the international community. It is a situation that is a source of growing concern to governments, economists and many business leaders, and not simply for ethical reasons. This growing divergence is dangerous.

Having countries that feel left behind as the world is getting richer it is not a situation we should stand by and watch. It could be a source of considerable instability. It is hard to imagine that the increasing inequality caused by globalization will not create increasing social unrest. It is not the only factor, of course, but it is definitely a driver.

---

[10] Heidelberg Institute on International Conflict Research (HIIK), 'Conflict Barometer 2005' (Heidelberg, 2005). http://www.hiik.de/en/index_e.htm

Benjamin Mkapa, the President of Tanzania, made the point even more bluntly in a recent interview. "Countries with impoverished, disadvantaged and desperate populations are breeding grounds for present and future terrorists," he said.[11]

Global military spending is rising dramatically, and is now at a level higher than the Cold War peak. There is a huge public commitment to end poverty worldwide and yet military spending remains a taboo subject.

World military spending has once again reached $ 1000 billion a year – even higher than it was at the height of the Cold War. The new 'long war' against terrorism is already several years old and shows no sign of ending soon. In fact, the new confrontations in the Middle East and elsewhere suggest that militarisation is on the increase as fresh conflicts loom over vital resources and holding back sustainable development.

Conflict tears families apart and splinters communities. It increases maternal mortality and the spread of disease. It destroys social infrastructure and makes work towards a better future, such as education, almost impossible. Conflict and lawlessness encourage criminality, deter investment and prevent normal economic activity. All this deepens and entrenches poverty.

Wars are often fought by people living on the margins: abducted children, or badly trained fighters. Poverty may cause conflict to continue when people – young men in particular – can find no alternative employment to fighting. In the absence of a reliable police force, communities may resort to paying racketeers to protect their

---

[11] See http://www.principalvoices.com/economy.html

families and businesses, even if that directly increases the resource base of warlords.[12]

## Interlinking 3 d's – disarmament, development, and democracy for a safer and sustainable world

Security is a fundamental prerequisite for development, which without peace, sustainable and broad-based development is not possible. In areas of conflict, it depends on the facilitation of sustainable reconstruction and development, including disarmament, demobilisation, reintegration and rehabilitation alongside the promotion of democracy, good governance and respect for human rights.

Disarmament, development and democracy are three of the international community's most important tools for building a world free from want and fear. By controlling or reducing the availability or use of the implements of armed violence and armed conflict, disarmament policies and programmes can facilitate a decrease in military expenditure, defuse tensions and encourage trust in inter-state and intra-state relations. The development of and spending on new weapons, incidence and severity of armed conflict and armed violence will have to stop for improving stability and freeing resources for other activities, such as economic and social development.

At the same time, by promoting economic and social progress and by generating opportunities for people, development policies and programmes can contribute to eradicating poverty, promoting economic growth and stabilising economies and states, thereby creating conditions of increased security and well being. Security and

---

[12] CAFOD, "The rough guide to conflict and peace policy," CAFOD briefing
   http://www.cafod.org.uk/policy_and_analysis/public_policy_papers/rough_guides

stability serve as the foundation for disarmament, development and democracy.

Although it was a decade of relative prosperity, the 1990s witnessed a widening global poverty gap, with enormous wealth concentrated in the hands of a few. Worldwide, the number of people living on less than $1 a day barely changed in the 1990s, and in some countries the situation has worsened. Globalisation has presented both opportunities and challenges for development; however, its costs and benefits have been unevenly distributed. The legacy of the cold war also had a damaging impact on the social and economic development of some States, in particular those highly indebted countries where a significant portion of national debt was incurred fighting the proxy wars of the bipolar conflict.

Underdevelopment and poverty continue to haunt a large number of nations. According to the United Nations Development Programme (UNDP) Human Development Report 2003, over 50 countries are poorer today than they were in 1990, human development indicators such as hunger, child mortality and primary school enrolment have worsened in some countries, and extreme poverty affects one fifth of humankind. In many countries, economic and social development has been thwarted by violent internal and regional conflicts, massive flows of refugees and internally displaced persons, problems of governance, illegal exploitation of conflict goods and natural resources, illicit trafficking of narcotics and weapons, and diseases such as HIV/AIDS.

With the end of the cold war, global military expenditure started to decrease. Many expected that this would result in a peace dividend as declining military spending and a less confrontational international environment would release financial, technological and human resources for development purposes. After the Cold War, in theory the peace dividend could have been obtained in a variety of forms,

# Fortune Forum Code

including trade expansion, efficient resource use, reduction of debt and technology transfer. This appears to have occurred in some countries, as the released resources fostered development through mechanisms such as research, investment, lower interest rates and economic growth. However, in practice, the peace dividend was not systematically and directly applied to development assistance for the world's poorest nations, nor did each country realise it in the same way.

The world's richest nations stand accused of double standards - exporting billions of pounds worth of arms to poor countries while discussing measures to lift them out of poverty. The pressure groups Oxfam and Amnesty International say the G8 countries are compounding the problems in developing nations, including much of Africa, by allowing them to import costly arms and weapons.

Britain is the world's second biggest arms supplier with exports estimated at $4.3bn (£2.2bn) between 1996 and 2003, less than America's $15.18bn but more than other G8 nations such as France ($3.02bn), Russia ($2.62bn) and Germany ($1.08bn). The 5 countries are the world's biggest arms exporters, accounting for 84 per cent of the global trade. Ironically, these are also the very countries that were at the G8 summit 2005, seeking to relieve global poverty in Africa, yet failing to understand the debilitating effect of the purchase of arms as it diverts resources in poor countries.

Many of the G8 countries are large donors to aid programmes in Africa and Asia. However, continuing arms transfers to developing countries undermine their pledges to relieve debt, combat Aids, alleviate poverty, tackle corruption and promote good governance. The arms can be used to suppress human rights and democracy.

According to Oxfam and Amnesty International, the G8 nations are not matching their rhetoric about arms sales and Africa with action.

"G8 governments have left significant loopholes in their own arms export standards and control mechanisms. Their efforts to control arms exports are not in proportion to the G8's global responsibility," the report says. It is difficult to take G8 commitments to end poverty and injustice seriously if some of the very same governments are undermining peace and stability by deliberately approving arms transfers to repressive regimes.[13]

Advancing human development requires governance that is democratic in both form and substance – for the people and by the people.

Democratic governance is valuable in its own right. But it can also advance human development, for three reasons. First, enjoying political freedom and participating in the decisions that shape one's life are fundamental human rights: they are part of human development in their own right. Democracy is the only political regime that guarantees political and civil freedoms and the right to participate – making democratic rule a good in itself.

Second, democracy helps protect people from economic and political catastrophes such as famines and descents into chaos. This is no small achievement. Indeed, it can mean the difference between life and death.

Democracies also contribute to political stability, providing open space for political opposition and handovers of power. Between 1950 and 1990 riots and demonstrations were more common in democracies but were much more destabilizing in dictatorships. Moreover, wars were more frequent in non-democratic regimes and

---

[13] The Independent, "Arms Trade undermines efforts to relieve debt" 22 June 2005 (London) See also "The G8: global arms exporters: failing to prevent irresponsible arms transfers" (2005).
http://www.oxfam.org/en/policy/briefingnotes/bpG8_ControlArms_050622.pdf

had much higher economic costs.

Third, democratic governance can trigger a virtuous cycle of development – as political freedom empowers people to press for policies that expand social and economic opportunities, and as open debates help communities shape their priorities.

Democracy that empowers people must be built – it cannot be imported. In many countries a central challenge for deepening democracy is building the key institutions of democratic governance:

• A system of representation, with well-functioning political parties and interest associations.

• An electoral system that guarantees free and fair elections as well as universal suffrage.

• A system of checks and balances based on the separation of powers, with independent judicial and legislative branches.

• A vibrant civil society, able to monitor government and private business - and provide alternative forms of political participation.

• A free, independent media.

• Effective civilian control over the military and other security forces.

These institutions come in many shapes and forms. Because the democracy a nation chooses to develop depends on its history and circumstances, countries will necessarily be "differently democratic". But in all countries democracy is about much more than a single decision or hastily organized election. It requires a deeper process of political development to embed democratic values and culture in all parts of society – a process never formally completed.

Building democratic institutions while achieving equitable social and economic development poses tensions. Granting all people formal political equality does not create an equal desire or capacity to participate in political processes – or an equal capacity to influence outcomes. Imbalances in resources and political power often subvert the principle of one person, one voice, and the purpose of democratic institutions. And judicial proceedings and regulatory institutions are undermined if elites dominate them at the expense of women, minorities and the powerless.

## UN initiatives and successes in peacekeeping

At the UN World Summit in September 2005 the leaders of 170 countries agreed a statement on a wide range of issues including development finance, the environment, and conflict. Despite polarised positions, they agreed two important issues for peace and conflict:

- A Peacebuilding Commission (PBC) was agreed in principle with two core objectives: to establish a UN body to help states avoid collapse or relapse into war, and to assist states in their transition from war to peace. The PBC would be responsible for marshalling resources and coordinating post-conflict reconstruction. It would be accompanied by a special new team of experts to help the Secretary General to mediate in more conflicts and bring them to a close.

- Responsibility to Protect (R2P) was endorsed in principle. This was a long overdue recognition that when a national government is unable or unwilling to protect its population from serious and irreparable harm – such as large-scale loss of life, ethnic cleansing, war crimes, widespread rape, or other acts of terror –

the international community must protect the population. It can use a range of responses: establishment of early warning systems, diplomatic mediation, and, as a last resort, military force under UN auspices. Prevention is the single most important dimension of R2P. Any military option should be used only after all diplomatic avenues are exhausted. This extreme option must have protection of civilians as its first objective and must follow precautionary principles such as ensuring that proportional means are used and that there is a reasonable prospect of success.

Some recent successes in peacekeeping and mediation

- In 2004, a total of 23 treaties or agreements were signed to regulate conflicts, 14 of them highly violent conflicts.[14]

- Mediation produced settlements in only about 25 per cent of civil wars, and only in those that attracted strong international support.[15]

- The UN Secretary General declared successful demobilisation of combatants to be the single most important factor in the success of peace operations.

## Turning good intentions into actions for development – debt relief, increased aid and fairer trade

On an international level, there are three key areas on which policy-makers are currently focusing in order to try to improve the lot of

---

[14] Heidelberg Institute on International Conflict Research (HIIK), "Conflict Barometer 2004", (Heidelberg, 2004). http://www.hiik.de/en/index_e.htm
[15] Ibid.

regions such as sub-Saharan Africa, and enable their citizens to claim a larger slice of the global economic cake.

The first is Third World debt relief. In many, if not most, developing countries, infrastructure improvement and economic growth are being stymied by the massive burden of international debt with which those countries are saddled. "The most indebted poor countries in the world currently owe a total of $375 billion," says The Jubilee Debt Campaign.[16]

Sub-Saharan Africa, the poorest region in the world, pays out $10 billion a year in debt servicing, about $27 million a day. In human development terms there is a desperate need for these countries to be able to spend their money on their own populations and infrastructure rather than paying it out to the rich world.

Another target area is the provision of foreign aid to developing countries. The amount of aid has been dropping steadily over the past few decades, and is according to the World Bank now at its lowest level since 1947 (0.22 percent of donor countries' GDP).

The US, one of the world's wealthiest countries, contributes just 0.1 percent of its GDP to foreign assistance, with a sizeable proportion of that taking the form of military aid to Israel and Egypt.

More financial aid is absolutely essential if we are to improve both human and physical infrastructure in these places. We need to make sure that more resources are made available to the developing world, and that those resources are used in an effective way.

Finally, there is a growing acceptance that economic liberalisation and free trade have been unfairly weighted in favour of the world's

---

[16] http://www.jubileedebtcampaign.org.uk

richer nations, who have been able to exploit global markets while at the same time resisting similar exploitation of their own markets.

In the US, for instance, the huge subsidies paid by the government to native cotton farmers - subsidies that, according to Oxfam, total more than the entire GDP of a country such as Burkina Faso - are denying the cotton producers of Africa and South America a level economic playing field on which to perform, driving many of them out of business.

If you are going to have globalisation it needs to be a two way street. Developing countries are opening up, but a lot of developed countries aren't. They have strong lobbies, especially in the agricultural sector, that are forcing governments to deny the liberalization to poorer nations.

We need to give developing countries far easier access to all global markets. Which is not necessarily the case today. Subsidies and market protection by high income countries are having a very negative impact. While taxation, debt relief, increased aid and fairer trade all have a role to play, however, there is also an awareness that the public sector alone cannot provide all the answers.

The role of the private sector is seen as equally if not more importantly in the struggle against inequality, helping to drive economic transformation from the bottom up, rather than vice versa. The Grameen Bank micro-credit system, for example, is a private sector initiative that has had an enormous effect on economic development by extending small loans to poor people - predominantly women - to enable them to start up and maintain their own businesses.

First established in Bangladesh in the 1970s by Mohammed Yunus, a US-educated Professor of Economics, the scheme has to date helped more than 16 million of the world's most disadvantaged people, both in developed and developing countries. Such has been the scheme's impact that the U.N. has declared 2005 The International Year of Micro-Credit.

The private sector is the single most influential factor in all of this. There is a huge market of people at the bottom of the social and economic pyramid who could be better served by businesses. Getting the domestic private sector to be aggressively looking for, and exploiting new opportunities is going to be very important for developing countries.

There are huge opportunities for these places to diversify into non-traditional exports. Flowers and organic fruits, for instance, are two products that would be ideally suited to East Africa. The basic infrastructure is needed but the private sector can play a huge role in the regeneration of struggling economies.

However, even with increased private sector involvement, there is considerable pessimism about whether any real change - "convergence" as it is sometimes called - will be achieved in the foreseeable future.

Vested interests in the developed world and chronic misgovernment and institutional weakness in many countries of the developing are just two of the factors hampering any attempt to create a fairer economic order.

There have been some successes. If you look at Asia, Eastern Europe and South America poverty levels have improved quite significantly. For the countries of Africa, on the other hand, it's going to take a huge amount of time to get anywhere close to the developed world.

To turn the situation around, the following actions are necessary:

# Fortune Forum Code

- calls for mainstreaming the disarmament-development relationship.

- raising awareness of this relationship within the international community.

- engaging in a wide range of conflict-prevention measures, including those related to illicit small arms and light weapons.

- promoting security through greater openness, transparency and confidence.

- strengthening further the role of the UN and other international institutions, as well as the donor community, towards these ends.

- the concept of human poverty as a complement to income poverty, emphasizing that equity, social inclusion, women's empowerment, and respect for human rights matter for poverty reduction.

- support efforts to build and strengthen democratic governance for achieving the twin pillars of stable societies – security and development.

- promote social coherence through civil society, development and multicultural tolerance.

- harness global science and technology to benefit the poor and bridging the digital divide.

- promote sustainable development for the adverse effects of environmental degradation related to industrial pollution, long term climate change, associated with massive use gas, oil and coal.

- empower individuals to take their destiny into their own hands for economic development and poverty reduction.

- The rule of law and adherence to multilateral treaties is a prerequisite for all nations. In its absence, wars and conflicts will be repeatedly waged at the cost of development.

## Progress towards Millennium Development Goals

Six years after world leaders committed themselves to a broad array of global goals, some progress has been made towards achieving the goals. It got slightly better at reducing hunger and extreme poverty, improving global public health, ensuring peace and security and providing access to basic education. Reports like the UN Millennium Project, the UK Africa Commission and the Millennium Ecosystem Assessment were produced.[17]

However, the power of inertia and shortsightedness remained. At the World Summit of almost all nations in September 2005, political leaders had the opportunity to commit themselves to a "grand bargain" that could have led to real breakthroughs on much of the global agenda, from development to security to human rights. They largely wasted the chance to dramatically improve the world but did reaffirm their commitment to creating a Peacebuilding Commission and the newly formed Human Rights Council.

The road to fight against AIDS requires a substantial amount of money but instead is largely filled with empty gestures. Global public health requires access to clean water and sanitation. Climate

---

[17] See Global Governance Initiative (2005), "Annual Report 2006," for the World Economic Forum, http://www.weforum.org/pdf/Initiatives/GGI_Report06.pdf

change is already exacerbating malaria, malnutrition and diarrhoea throughout the world. The world's poorest people need sustainable managed ecosystems to preserve their livelihoods, and the scarcity of natural resources can fuel violent conflict. Making the transition from talking to acting matters not only because of the inherent importance of these issues, but because progress in one area depends so heavily on progress in the others.

Some hope may be taken from the positive role played by non-state actors. Civil society groups mobilised on an unprecedented scale to force governments to get more serious about their commitments to the world's poor. Local and regional governments did more than their national counterparts to reduce greenhouse gas emissions. Businesses are conscious with notions of social responsibility, and private foundations and pharmaceutical firms now account for an enormous share of the progress on global public health.

Overall, the period since the Millennium Declaration has been filled with grand opportunities and inadequate actions, leaving ever more riding on what the world can muster the courage to do in 2006 and beyond. We do not yet know whether the slight improvement in several of the scores in the past year is a blip in a continuing cycle of neglect and apathy, or the start of a serious trend toward real progress in the human condition.

**Four pillars of cooperation**

The completion of the MDGs should focus on four pillars of cooperation, each in urgent need of renovation.

- The first pillar is development assistance.

International aid is a key investment in human development. Returns to that investment can be measured in the human potential unleashed by averting avoidable sickness and deaths, educating all children, overcoming gender inequalities and creating the conditions for sustained economic growth. Development assistance suffers from two problems: chronic underfinancing and poor quality. There have been improvements on both fronts. But much remains to be done to close the MDG financing gaps and improve value for money.[18]

- The second pillar is international trade.

Under the right conditions, trade can be a powerful catalyst for human development. The Doha "Development Round" of World Trade Organisation (WTO) talks, launched in 2001, provided rich country governments with an opportunity to create those conditions. This was the moment to prove that the Millennium Declaration is not just a paper promise, but a commitment to change.

We know now nothing of substance has been achieved. Rich country trade policies continue to deny poor countries and poor people a fair share of global prosperity—and they fly in the face of the Millennium Declaration. More than aid, trade has the potential to increase the share of the world's poorest countries and people in global prosperity. Limiting that potential through unfair trade policies is inconsistent with a commitment to the MDGs. More than that, it is unjust and hypocritical.

- The third pillar is security.

Violent conflict blights the lives of hundreds of millions of people. It is a source of systematic violations of human rights and a barrier to progress towards the MDGs. The nature of conflict has changed, and new threats to collective security have emerged. In an increasingly

---

[18] UNDP (2003) "Human Development Report 2005", New York
http://hdr.undp.org/reports/global/2005/

# Fortune Forum Code

interconnected world the threats posed by a failure to prevent conflict, or to seize opportunities for peace, inevitably cross national borders. More effective international cooperation could help to remove the barrier to MDG progress created by violent conflict, creating the conditions for accelerated human development and real security.

- The fourth pillar is global education.

Despite the efforts of the international community, over 800 million people in the world cannot read or write, and more than 100 million children (55% of whom are girls) are unable to attend school. In many low-income countries teachers are not qualified for their jobs, and many are not well versed in study programs.

As for information technologies, less than 10% of the world's population has access to the Internet, and 70% have never even heard of it. Moreover, the development of the world economic space and the ensuing globalisation of the labour market are turning recognition of professional skills and comparison of national education systems into a major challenge.

Peace education is non-existent in schools and universities. However it is key for an ethical foundation of our society and to protect core values of life - freedom, equality, solidarity, tolerance, respect for nature, shared responsibility and multiculturalism.

It is important to:

- promote the system of continuing education;
- make primary education universal in developing nations;
- raise the quality of education;
- expand international exchanges of students, professors and researchers;

# Vijay Mehta

- help develop distance learning and ICT (Information and Communication Technology) in primary, secondary, and vocational education.
- promote a culture of peace and peace education in developing and developed countries.

# 3
# Africa – A Special Case

---

*Can there be an African miracle?*

## Introduction[19]

*African poverty and stagnation is the greatest tragedy of our time. Poverty on such a scale demands a forceful response. And Africa – at country, regional, and continental levels – is creating much stronger foundations for tackling its problems. Recent years have seen improvements in economic growth and in governance. But Africa needs more of both if it is to make serious inroads into poverty. To do that requires a partnership between Africa and the developed world which takes full account of Africa's diversity and particular circumstances.*

For its part, Africa must accelerate reform. And the developed world must increase and improve its aid, and stop doing those things which hinder Africa's progress. The developed world has a moral duty – as well as a powerful motive of self-interest – to assist Africa. We believe that now is the time when greater external support can have a major impact and this is a vital moment for the world to get behind Africa's efforts.

## Getting systems right: governance and capacity-building

Africa's history over the last fifty years has been blighted by two areas of weakness. These have been capacity – the ability to design

---

[19] See Commission for Africa (2005), http://www.commissionforafrica.org/

and deliver policies; and accountability – how well a state answers to its people. Improvements in both are first and foremost the responsibility of African countries and people. But action by rich nations is essential too.

Building capacity takes time and commitment. Weak capacity is a matter of poor systems and incentives, poor information, technical inability, untrained staff and lack of money. We recommend that donors make a major investment to improve Africa's capacity, starting with its system of higher education, particularly in science and technology. They must help to build systems and staff in national and local governments, but also in pan-African and regional organisations, particularly the African Union and its NEPAD[20] programme. Donors must change their behaviour and support the national priorities of African governments rather than allowing their own procedures and special enthusiasms to undermine the building of a country's own capacity.

Improving accountability is the job of African leaders. They can do that by broadening the participation of ordinary people in government processes, in part by strengthening institutions like parliaments, local authorities, trades unions, the justice system and the media. Donors can help with this. They can also help build accountable budgetary processes so that the people of Africa can see how money is raised and where it is going. That kind of transparency can help combat corruption, which African governments must root out. Developed nations can help in this too. Money and state assets stolen from the people of Africa by corrupt leaders must be repatriated. Foreign banks must be obliged by law to inform on suspicious accounts. Those who give bribes should be dealt with too; and foreign companies involved in oil, minerals and other extractive industries must make their payments much more open to public

---

[20] New Economic Programme for Africa's Development.

scrutiny. Firms who bribe should be refused export credits. Without progress in governance, all other reforms will have limited impact.

## The need for peace and security

The most extreme breakdown of governance is war. Africa has experienced more violent conflict than any other continent in the last four decades. In recent years things have improved in many countries, but in other places violent conflict is still the biggest single obstacle to development. Investing in development is investing in peace.

The most effective way to tackle conflict – to save both lives and money – is to build the capacity of African states and societies to prevent and manage conflict. That means using aid better to tackle the causes of conflict. It means improving the management of government incomes from natural resources and international agreements on how to control the 'conflict resources' which fuel or fund hostilities. It means controlling the trade in small arms.

African regional organisations and the UN can help prevent and resolve conflict when tensions cannot be managed at the national level, through, for example, effective early warning, mediation and peacekeeping. Donors can support this by providing flexible funding to the African Union and the continent's regional organisations; and supporting the creation of a UN Peacebuilding Commission. The co-ordination and financing of postconflict, peacebuilding and development must be improved to prevent states emerging from violent conflict from sliding back into it.

# Vijay Mehta

## Leaving no-one out: investing in people

Poverty is more than just a lack of material things. Poor people are excluded from decision-making and from the basic services the state ought to provide. Schools and clinics must be available to the poorest people in Africa. This is an urgent matter of basic human rights and social justice. But it is also sound economics: a healthy and skilled workforce is a more productive one, fulfilling their potential with dignity. Investing for economic growth means rebuilding African health and education systems, many of which are now on the point of collapse. This requires major funding, but it is not only a question of resources. It is also about delivery and results. These are powerfully strengthened when local communities are involved in decisions that affect them.

Properly funding the international community's commitment to Education for All will provide all girls and boys in sub-Saharan Africa with access to basic education to equip them with skills for contemporary Africa. Secondary, higher and vocational education, adult learning, and teacher training should also be supported within a balanced overall education system. Donors need to pay what is needed to deliver their promises – including the cost of removing primary school fees.

The elimination of preventable diseases in Africa depends above all on rebuilding systems to deliver public health services in order to tackle diseases such as TB and malaria effectively. This will involve major investment in staff, training, the development of new medicines, better sexual and reproductive health services and the removal of fees paid by patients, which should be paid for by donors until countries can afford it. Funding for water supply and sanitation should be immediately increased, reversing years of decline. Top priority must be given to scaling up the services needed to deal with the catastrophe of HIV and AIDS which is killing more people in

Africa than anywhere else in the world. But this must be done through existing systems, rather than parallel new ones. Governments should also be supported to protect orphans and vulnerable children and other groups who would otherwise be left out of the growth story. Around half of the extra aid we are recommending should be spent on health, education and HIV and AIDS.

## Going for growth and poverty reduction

Africa is poor, ultimately, because its economy has not grown. The public and private sectors need to work together to create a climate which unleashes the entrepreneurship of the peoples of Africa, generates employment and encourages individuals and firms, domestic and foreign, to invest. Changes in governance are needed to make the investment climate stronger. The developed world should support the African Union's NEPAD programme to build public/private partnerships in order to create a stronger climate for growth, investment and jobs.

Growth will also require a massive investment in infrastructure to break down the internal barriers that hold Africa back. Donors should fund a doubling of spending on infrastructure – from rural roads and small-scale irrigation to regional highways, railways, larger power projects and Information & Communications Technology (ICT). That investment must include both rural development and slum upgrading, without which the poor people in Africa will not be able to participate in growth. And policies for growth must actively include – and take care not to exclude – the poorest groups. There should be particular emphasis on agriculture and on helping small enterprises, with a particular focus on women and young people. For growth to be sustainable, safeguarding the environment and addressing the risks of climate change should be integral to donor and government programmes. This programme for growth takes over a third of the total additional resources we propose.

## More trade and fairer trade

Africa faces two major constraints on trade. It does not produce enough goods, of the right quality or price, to enable it to break into world markets. And it faces indefensible trade barriers which, directly or indirectly, tax its goods as they enter the markets of developed countries.

To improve its capacity to trade Africa needs to make changes internally. It must improve its transport infrastructure to make goods cheaper to move. It must reduce and simplify the tariff systems between one African country and another. It must reform excessive bureaucracy, cumbersome customs procedures, and corruption by public servants, wherever these exist. It must make it easier to set up businesses. It must improve economic integration within the continent's regional economic communities. Donors can help fund these changes.

But the rich nations must also dismantle the barriers they have erected against African goods, particularly in agriculture. These barriers hurt citizens in both rich and poor countries. Rich countries must abolish trade-distorting subsidies to their agriculture and agribusiness which give them an unfair advantage over poor African farmers. They should lower tariffs and other non-tariff barriers to African products, including stopping the bureaucratic application of rules of origin which excludes African goods from preferences to which they are entitled. And they should show this ambition by completing of world trade talks in a way which does not demand reciprocal concessions from poor African nations. Careful attention should be given to ensure that the poorest people are helped to take advantage of the new opportunities and to cope with the impacts of a more open system of world trade. Africa should be provided with the funds that can help it adjust to the new opportunities of a changed world trading regime.


## Where will the money come from: resources

To support the changes that have begun in Africa, there should be available an additional US$25 billion per year in aid, to be implemented by 2010. Donor countries should commit immediately to provide their fair share of this. Subject to a review of progress then, there would be a second stage, with a further US$25 billion a year to be implemented by 2015. Ensuring the money is well spent will depend on two factors. First, good governance in Africa must continue to advance. But, second, donors must significantly improve the quality of aid and how it is delivered: that means more grants, more predictable and untied aid, and donor processes that are less burdensome on the already stretched administrations of African countries. It should also be better harmonised with the aid of other donors and better in line with the priorities, procedures and systems of African governments. Above all, it should be given in ways that make governments answerable primarily to their own people.

These changes are needed not just from individual donor nations but also from multilateral institutions – both African and global. The African Development Bank needs to be strengthened and the role of the Economic Commission for Africa enhanced. The IMF and World Bank need to give higher priority to Africa's development. They also need to become more accountable both to their shareholders and to their clients, and to give Africa a stronger voice in their decision-making.

Rich nations should commit to a timetable for giving 0.7 per cent of their annual income in aid. To provide the critical mass of aid which is needed now, the aid should be front-loaded through the immediate implementation of the International Finance Facility. Practical proposals should be developed for innovative financing methods such as international levies on aviation, which can help secure funding for the medium and longer term.

For poor countries in sub-Saharan Africa which need it, the objective must be 100 per cent debt cancellation as soon as possible. This should be part of a financing package for these countries – including those excluded from current debt schemes – to achieve the Millennium Development Goals to halve world poverty by 2015, as promised by the international community at meetings in Monterrey (Mexico) and Kananaskis (Canada).

**Conclusion**

Bold comprehensive action on a scale needed to meet the challenges can only be done through a new kind of partnership. In the past, contractual and conditional approaches were tried, and failed. What we are suggesting is a new kind of development, based on mutual respect and solidarity, and rooted in a sound analysis of what actually works. This can speed up progress, building on recent positive developments in Africa, towards a just world, of which, Africa is an integral part.

# 4
# Environmental Sustainability

*Can the world be saved from climate change?*

## Introduction

According to data gathered by the UN, the number of major natural disasters – cyclones, droughts, floods, avalanches, forest fires, tidal waves and earthquakes – has increased fourfold during the last 30 years. At this pace, some 2 million more people are likely to be displaced each year on account of natural catastrophes. One heat wave alone killed 20,000 people in Europe. The increase in size, duration and power of tropical storms and hurricanes is being linked to global warming. Climate change is owing to human emissions of greenhouse gases, and thus is causing more frequent floods and droughts.

The planet is warming rapidly. Arctic ice is at record lows and the North Pole could melt to open water sometime this century for the first time in some 40 million years. The mighty Antarctic ice sheet is creaking and dramatic changes are expected, from the Amazon rainforest to the Siberian permafrost.

Increasing depletion of fossil fuel energy (4.3% increase in 2004) has swelled carbon emissions in the atmosphere. The original target of reducing emissions by 5%, under the Kyoto Protocol, looks unrealistic. We can explore how sustainable land-use practices, to sequester carbon (carbon trading), can work to shift the destruction paradigm between forest communities, their environment and the need for food security and income. Carbon trading puts a tangible price tag on environmental pollution.

Environmental degradation and natural resource depletion continues unabated threatening our natural systems and resources, for our existence and development. Desertification, lack of biodiversity, forest loss, reduced stock of marine fisheries and the depletion of the ozone layer continue to pose risks for the global environment.

Travel is the cause of nine-tenths of carbon-monoxide emissions, three-quarters of nitrogen oxide emissions of known origin, and one-third of the particles emitted into the atmosphere. Car exhaust emissions account for one-half of urban pollution and over one-quarter of greenhouse effect emissions. The World Bank assesses at 1.56 million deaths per year the cost to Asia of atmospheric pollution.

More than 1.5 billion people does not have direct access to drinking water and more than half of humanity does not have access to satisfactory water purification plants. Although two-thirds of our planet is water, less than one-half of 1 per cent is available fresh water. The health and economic development of a nation will be significantly endangered with the looming scarcity of clean water in certain regions of the world. It is estimated that by 2050, over 800 million people will be severely affected which may turn into conflicts in a similar way as we see the fight for valuable resources, such as oil and diamonds. The problem is not so much water shortage on a world scale as the inequality of its distribution.

**A year of disasters**

For too many people, 2005 will be remembered for its disasters. Around the Indian Ocean, communities and governments struggled to rebuild after the 26 December 2004 earthquake, which measured more than 9.1 on the Richter scale, and the subsequent tsunami, which claimed more than 250,000 lives in 12 countries. In August 2005, hurricanes swept through the Gulf Coast of the United States, taking more than 1,000 lives and inflicting billions of dollars worth of damage. In October 2005, a magnitude 7.6 earthquake shook South Asia, at a cost of more than 70,000 lives, mostly in Pakistan, with millions more exposed to harsh winter conditions. Other disasters included floods in Switzerland, a chemical spill in China and swarms of locusts in Africa. All had severe consequences for lives and livelihoods.

There might be debate about the precise extent of the problem, the timescales involved, and the most effective solution. On the over-arching issue, however, a clear majority of the world's scientific experts are in agreement: Our natural environment is in trouble – and the trouble is getting worse as each year passes.

They argue that global climate change, pollution of water, land and air, loss of habitat, diminution of natural resources and species extinction, all are the result of human activity. All are accelerating, and are inexorably making our world a more difficult, less accommodating place in which to live.

The statistics are plentiful, and alarming. According to the United Nations Environmental Programme (UNEP), 15 million hectares of tropical rainforest - an area the size of England and Wales - is being lost each year to the logging industry.

It says 12,000 cubic kilometres of water worldwide are dangerously polluted - more than the total amount of water contained in the world's 10 largest river basins - and 11,000 species of animal and plant are under threat of extinction, a level not seen since the age of the dinosaurs.

# Vijay Mehta

Most worrying of all, many scientists say the 6.6 billion metric tonnes of carbon dioxide our factories, transport systems and power stations pump into the atmosphere annually are having a potentially catastrophic effect on the earth's climate. Thereby, increasing global warming and leading to ever more extreme weather events.

Most scientists agree that we will be experiencing serious environmental problems within the next few decades, and that those problems will need careful management. While there is broad consensus on the need for action, however, there is also awareness that a "stop the world I want to get off" philosophy is simply not practical in the modern industrial age.

In developing countries in particular, environmental degradation is, to a greater or lesser extent, an inevitable by-product of economic growth – growth that is essential if those countries are ever to alleviate the poverty in which a majority of their citizens exist.

The question facing the world's governments, businesses and green groups is thus not simply how best to tackle the world's growing environmental crisis, but how to do so in a manner that does not at the same time hamstring national economies, especially those of the world's poorest nations.

## Placing the environmental issues on the global agenda

In short, as we move into the 21st century, how can the human race achieve the goal of sustainable development? The 1972 United Nations Stockholm Conference is generally seen as the watershed. While there were regional initiatives before that, it was essentially Stockholm that started the whole environmental ball rolling.

# Fortune Forum Code

The conference was the first of its kind to unequivocally acknowledge that human activity was seriously damaging the world's natural environment, and to propose a series of measures – both national and global – to try and tackle the problem. As its final Declaration read:

"A point has been reached in history when we must shape our actions throughout the world with a more prudent care for their environmental consequences."

In the same year, four young scientists at the Massachusetts Institute of Technology produced a controversial report titled "The Limits To Growth," using computer models to smash the long-held assumption that the Earth's resources could support limitless economic growth and population expansion. Their findings caused a sensation, selling 12 million copies and added weight to calls for an urgent global strategy to safeguard the environment.

In the 30 years since those two landmark events there have been a succession of conferences, summits and initiatives aimed at building on the foundations laid in 1972. The 1992 U.N. Conference on Environment and Development in Rio de Janeiro, the 1997 Kyoto Protocol, and the 2002 Johannesburg World Summit on Sustainable Development have all sought to highlight the problems facing our natural environment, and to implement measures to try to alleviate those problems.

Their remit has covered everything from the provision of clean drinking water to the protection of endangered species, the disposal of domestic waste to the promotion of lead-free petrol. Above all they have sought to address the problem of global warming and climate change, considered by most experts to be the defining environmental issue of our age, and the one that presents the greatest challenge to the goal of sustainable development.

# Vijay Mehta

## Facts, forecasts and impacts[21]

- The 1990s was the warmest decade, and 1998 the warmest year on global record (Intergovernmental Panel on Climate Change, IPCC).
- The Earth is warming faster than at any time in the past 10,000 years (IPCC).
- The burning of coal, oil and gas has increased the amount of $CO^2$ in the atmosphere by 30% over natural levels (IPCC).
- The summer of 2003 was Europe's hottest for 500 years. The heatwave caused 28,000 premature deaths across the continent.
- Europe's capitals have warmed, some by 2°C in the last 30 years. London's average maximum summer temperature increased the most. This warming trend will increase the likelihood of more frequent and intense heatwaves, droughts and rainstorms (World Wildlife Federation-UK).
- One hundred and fifty thousand people already die every year from climate change (World Health Organisation).
- The area of the world stricken by drought has doubled between 1970 and the early 2000s (Greenpeace).
- The economic costs of global warming are doubling every decade (UN).
- The impact of climate change on some wildlife will already be catastrophic even with little further change in the climate. Up to a third of land-based species could face extinction by the middle of the century (Royal Society for the Protection of Birds).
- One hundred million more people will be flooded by the end of the century (Friends of the Earth).
- People in low-income countries are four times more likely to die in natural disasters than people in high income countries. Globally, disaster losses increased from $71 billion in the 1960s

---

[21] Facts and forecasts were taken from www.stopclimatechaos.org.uk

to $608 billion in 1990s. Poverty and lagging development exacerbates people's vulnerability to extreme weather (Oxfam).

- Water availability could decline – over 3 billion people in the Middle East and the Indian sub-continent could be facing acute shortages of water (Oxfam).
- Global warming will submerge many low-lying island nations entirely – one of the Carteret atolls of Papua New Guinea has already been cut in half by the ocean. Tuvalu in the South Pacific has concluded a deal with New Zealand to evacuate the entire 10,000 population (People & Planet).
- There has been a 40% drop in the amount of Arctic ice since the 1970s. Were this effect to spread, and the northern ice fields melt, a rise in sea levels of up to 7 meters would occur. This would not simply overwhelm low-lying countries like Bangladesh, but also major western cities such as London, Rome and New York (People & Planet).
- The whole western Siberian sub-Arctic region has started to thaw for the first time since its formation, 11,000 years ago. The area, which is the size of France and Germany combined, could release billions of tonnes of greenhouse gases into the atmosphere. This would be irreversible and would ramp up temperatures even more (BBC).
- In the next 15 years, displacement, disruption to agriculture and food supplies, and damage and destruction to infrastructure would be likely to lead to economic and political instability, both within countries and across international borders, and even to wars as environmental refugees seek new homes, and countries clash over scarce water and food supplies. The industrial countries also could find themselves under immense pressure from huge numbers of environmental refugees from the developing world (Christian Aid).
- By the end of the century, rising sea levels and crop failures could create 150 million refugees. Even in the UK, 5 million people are at risk from increased flood and storm damage

# Vijay Mehta

(Operation Noah).

- In one region of Mozambique, it used to be normal to have two seasons – hot and cool. Recently temperatures have risen from 30°C up to 49°C in the hot season and are less cold in the cool season, changing the timing of the rains. The majority of communities are afraid to plant, thinking that it is not the right time, thus affecting the food security of the region (Tearfund).
- The cost of insured damage in a severe hurricane season in the USA could rise by three-quarters to £82billion ($ 150 billion), an increase equivalent to almost three Hurricane Andrews – the costliest single weather event recorded" (Association of British Insurers).
- The financial costs of flooding could rise in both the UK and the rest of Europe, increasing the annual flood bill by up to £82 billion across Europe (Association of British Insurers).

## Global warming

It is incontrovertible that the burning of fossil fuels is altering the chemistry of the atmosphere and there is compelling evidence that that is causing climate change. The effects of climate change are already apparent, with increasing incidence of floods, storms, droughts, water shortages and rising sea levels; phenomena that are expected to grow in severity over the course of the next century, and which are likely to hit the world's poorest countries hardest.

"Africa is the prime example," says Nick Nuttall of the United Nations Environment Programme. "The continent accounts for only 3 percent of all global warming emissions, yet it suffers the most from the effects of global warming because its countries don't have the finance or infrastructure to combat those effects."

# Fortune Forum Code

Dr. Rajendra Pachauri, chair of the UN's Intergovernmental Panel on Climate Change, concurs: "The impacts of climate change fall disproportionately on the poor. Farmers in tropical and sub-tropical countries are dependent on rains. Variations in rainfall and increased frequency of extreme weather conditions could make the lot of peasants far more difficult than it is currently," he says.

The 1997 Kyoto Protocol was an ambitious attempt to get to grips with the problem, committing the world's 38 largest industrialised countries to specific targets for reducing their 1990 levels of greenhouse gas emissions. Thus the US, which has 4 percent of the world's population, yet is responsible for 25 percent of all global carbon emissions, agreed to cut those emissions by 7 percent, Britain by 12.5 per cent and Germany by 21 per cent. At the same time, poorer countries such as India and China, both of which are set to become major polluters over the next 30 years, were given a moratorium on reducing greenhouse gases to allow their economies to develop and grow.

Despite its good intentions, however, the initiative is already in trouble as America withdrew from the Protocol in March 2001. Russia's recent decision to ratify the treaty means that it has come into force and will be operative.[22] There are those who argue that even if it does, that will still not be enough to slow, let alone halt or reverse, the global warming bandwagon.

It's a huge problem and something needs to be done. The whole thing is mixed up with our lifestyles and aspirations and patterns of energy use. There's just no obvious fix to all of this.

---

[22] To be legally binding it needs to be ratified by countries that together were responsible for at least 55 percent of the total 1990 greenhouse gas emissions

# Vijay Mehta

## Information for decision-making[23]

Reversing climate change, and mitigating or adapting to its effects, needs the active collaboration of governments, the private sector and civil society. Governments are directly responsible for only a small proportion of greenhouse gas emissions, therefore they must persuade businesses, communities and individuals to adjust their activities in order to limit emissions and promote adaptation. They have several tools at their disposal for achieving this. Policies can be used to raise the cost of activities that emit greenhouse gases or prevent adaptation and reduce the costs of activities that do not; regulations and standards can mandate changes in products and practices; taxes and subsidies can be adjusted to influence behaviour.

Such measures, however, can generate considerable opposition. Education, training and public awareness – the subject of Article 6 of the Climate Change Convention – is therefore vital for generating support for such policies. UNEP works closely with the Climate Change Convention and the Intergovernmental Panel on Climate Change (IPCC) on climate outreach. The IPCC, established in 1988 by UNEP and the World Meteorological Organization (WMO), is the world's most authoritative scientific source of climate change information. Its assessments provided an essential basis for the negotiation of the Climate Change Convention and the Kyoto Protocol. [24]

## Environment for a secure future

Environmental problems related to human activities – such as climate

---

[24] UNEP (2004), "UNEP Annual Report 2004," see 'Combating Climate Change,' http://www.unep.org/Documents.Multilingual/Default.asp?DocumentID=67

change, water scarcity and land degradation – are among the most powerful and least understood challenges for sustainable development. There is a growing consensus that these issues can also be flashpoints for confrontation between communities and even nations.

*Adapting to climate change*
The latest data shows that greenhouse gas emissions continue to rise. Furthermore, concentrations of carbon dioxide in the atmosphere rose by a record amount in 2004 – the third successive year that carbon dioxide levels have increased sharply. The countries most vulnerable to climate change are the least developed countries and Small Island Developing States.

*Clean and renewable energy*
According to the UN Secretary-General's High-Level Panel on Threats, Challenges and Change, "modern economies need to reduce their dependence on hydrocarbons and should undertake a special effort to devise climate friendly development strategies," to address problems of climate change. States should provide incentives for the further development of renewable energy sources and begin to phase out environmentally harmful subsidies, especially for fossil fuel use and development.

UNEP's Energy Programme addresses the environmental consequences of energy production and use, such as global climate change and local air pollution. It has two areas of focus: promoting policies that place energy and transport within a broader sustainable development context, and steering project developers and the investment community towards greater support for renewable energy and energy efficiency projects. With its two collaborating centres – the UNEP Risoe Centre on Energy, Climate and Sustainable Development, and the Basel Agency for Sustainable Energy (BASE), UNEP is working with a wide range of stakeholders to diversify and increase the global share of renewable energy sources, improve access to environmentally sound energy resources and services, remove market distortions, provide access to energy markets, and accelerate the development and dissemination of better energy efficiency methods and technology.

One of the most significant energy events of the year was the International Conference on Renewable Energies 2004, held in June in Bonn, Germany. The Conference was one of the largest intergovernmental gatherings of its type, attracting more than 3,000 participants from 154 countries. UNEP hosted a number of side events, press conferences and an exhibition stand, as well as the two-day event, Financing Sustainable Energy: Creating the Climate for Change, as part of the new Sustainable Energy Finance Initiative.

The event created a forum for 275 representatives from the finance, business and government sectors to discuss actions needed to increase investment in the renewable energy and energy efficiency sectors. The meeting featured sessions organised by leading financial institutions on topics such as venture capital, infrastructure, consumer and carbon finance, export credits and risk management. Also at the Bonn event, the fifth BASE International Investment Forum for Sustainable Energy presented a range of companies and investment vehicles raising capital for sustainable energy ventures.

*Sustainable energy solutions*
UNEP's Rural Energy Enterprise Development (REED) programme was also recognized during the Bonn Conference as a progressive model for sustainable development. Its portfolio in Africa and Brazil continues to grow, with $1 million currently invested in 24 enterprises. One of its major development, during the year, was the production of The REED Toolkit, a step-by-step guide for turning a clean energy business idea into a reality.

# Fortune Forum Code

Another sustainable energy example is UNEP's Indian Solar Loan Programme. After its first year, the programme has disbursed almost 5,000 loans for photovoltaic-based Solar Home Systems, expanded to 1,800 participating bank branches, and remains on target to deliver clean electricity to up to 25,000 Indian families by 2006. It offers a credit facility with two of India's largest banks, Canara Bank and Syndicate Bank (and their Grameen Banks). The basis of the programme is a progressively decreasing interest rate subsidy over time that acts to lower the commercial lending rate from 12 per cent to 5 per cent. The programme, which has exceeded UNEP's initial benchmark, demonstrates the need for new finance products to develop renewable energy markets.

In North Africa, a partnership between UNEP, the Tunisian state utility, STEG, and the Agence Nationale pour la Maîtrise de l'Energie, has launched SOLdinars, a solar loan facility to help tens of thousands of Tunisian households acquire solar water heating. With funding from the Italian government and as part of the Mediterranean Renewable Energy Programme, SOLdinars enhances credit through an interest rate subsidy on loans from local banks where repayments are made via STEG utility bills, reducing the credit risk for the banks and allowing them to further lower interest premiums to 4 per cent. Another finance programme is under development for solar water heating in 200 North African hotels.

## Some improvement

But it is not all bad news. If global warming remains, for the present at least, a seemingly intractable issue, advances are being made in other areas. The world is clearly far more aware of environmental issues than it was 30 years ago. Around the world, a whole plethora of initiatives, some driven by national governments, most originating at a local government or community level, are helping to improve the environment and preserve it for future generations.

For example, in Brazil, the Municipality of Porto Allegre has launched the Guaiba Lives Programme, involving the local community and public authorities in an ambitious scheme to clean up Guaiba Lake, upon which Porto Allegre depends for its water supply.

New sewage treatment plants have been built, a water treatment facility installed, environmental education classes set up, and shanty-dwellers along the lakeshore resettled. The result has been a dramatic improvement in the lake's water quality and biodiversity.

In the US, meanwhile, Xerox has pioneered the concept of the "backtrack" factory. Rather than simply throwing out Xerox products when they have reached their sell-by date, the company's clients can now return those products to the factory for updating, thus cutting waste and conserving resources.

While such schemes are helping to improve the environment, however, they are, in the end, just a drop in the ocean. Even in the developed world, while there are clear signs of improvement, most of the consumption and production patters that cause environmental problems have stayed the same, or if anything, intensified.

## Need for new initiatives in urban areas

Urban areas are responsible for more than 75 per cent of all greenhouse gas emissions, making reduced energy crucial in the effort to slow the pace of global warming.

Energy-efficient traffic lights, street lighting, the use of biofuels for city transport, and traffic congestion schemes were some of the practical steps that cities are expected to take to reduce greenhouse gases. The world's largest cities can have a major impact on this. Already they are developing the technologies and innovative new practices that provide hope that we can radically reduce carbon emissions. [25]


## Energy security

Reliable and adequate energy supply is key to the socio-economic development of mankind. The existing energy networks have become highly integrated and have achieved global scale, which is a positive trend. Unfortunately, the failure of one element in a highly integrated network inevitably affects the others. Parochial national efforts to ensure energy security have so far proved unsuccessful. A global challenge calls for concerted global action.

The known hydrocarbon resources and the existing investment and technological capabilities are sufficient to ensure the reliable and affordable supply of adequate amount of energy in the foreseeable future. This, however, will only come through an efficient system of global, regional, and local markets, in which the role of governments would be to set the rules, defend and protect key energy facilities, insure against market failures, stimulate technological innovation, and ensure environmental sustainability of energy development.

Sustainable global energy security requires security of demand as well as of supply, which, in turn, implies a need for more transparent and predictable activities at the level of statistics and energy policies. This tremendous objective will be achieved through further producer-consumer dialogue, fair distribution of investment risks, and mutual openness to capital. More transparent, predictable, and stable energy markets are the key to success.

---

[25] Environmental News Network, "Major world cities team up to fight global warming", 4 August 2006

# Vijay Mehta

Predictable government regulation in producer, transporter, and consumer countries will stimulate energy investment – provided multilateral market tools are effective enough and such key prerequisites as clear investment frameworks, consistent taxation, minimization of red tape, timely and full enforcement of contracts, and access to workable dispute settlement procedures be in place.

In stimulating investment, an important thing to look at is different investment sensitivity at the sending as well as at the receiving end of the energy train. Possible ways to balance it off are long-term contracts and producer-consumer interdependence achieved, for example, through asset swaps.

Energy efficiency and energy saving represent another crucial dimension of global security as they help decrease power consumption, thus alleviating energy tensions. This objective can be achieved through national and multilateral energy intensity statistics, shared information of energy saving targets, comprehensive power consumption identification, and enforcement of energy efficiency standards.

In the energy industry, higher energy efficiency comes hand-in-hand with lesser impact on the environment. In this light, the industry is planning new efforts to increase oil and gas recovery, oil refinement ratio, petroleum gas utilisation, and infrastructure reliability. Energy saving will become a priority issue for transportation, a sector responsible for two-thirds of global oil consumption.

Energy security will not become a reality without diversification, which, most importantly, means the expansion of types of energy in use into low-carbon alternative power, renewables, and innovations for conventional energy sectors. Nuclear energy is also a way but it requires appreciable efforts to ensure safety, environmental accountability, and rigorous international monitoring.

Diversification will also be promoted by an effort maintained by G8-encouraged international partnerships working on carbon capture, hydrogen economy, ITER[26] and other projects.

Lastly, global energy security will only be possible provided two major international challenges – climate change and access of poorest people in developing nations to modern energy services – are properly addressed.

## Rich and poor countries face water crisis[27]

Rich countries have to make drastic changes to policies if they are to avoid the water crisis that is facing poorer nations. The industrialised world in many cities are already losing the battle to maintain water supplies as governments talk about conservation but fail to implement their pledges. Supporting large-scale industry and growing populations using water at high rates has come close to exhausting the water supplies of some First World cities and is a looming threat for many.

The agriculture in the richer countries should have to pay more for water and be held responsible more actively for its efficient use and for managing wastes, like salt, especially in intensive livestock farming.

From Seville in Spain to Sacramento in California and Sydney in Australia, water has become a key political issue at local, regional and national levels as climate change and loss of wetlands

---

[26] ITER was originally an acronym standing for International Thermonuclear Experimental Reactor.

[27] Environmental News Network, "Rich countries like poor face water crisis", 16 August 2006

dramatically reduce supplies.

It is now generally accepted in the developed world that water must be used more efficiently and that water must be made available again to the environment in sufficient quantity for natural systems to function.

Many countries also recognise that extensive - and very expensive - repairs are required to reduce some of the damage inflicted on water systems and catchments in the past.

Putting the rhetoric into practice in the face of habitual practices and intense lobbying by vested interests has been very difficult.

In Europe, countries around the Atlantic are suffering from recurring droughts, while in the Mediterranean region water resources were being depleted by the boom in tourism and irrigated agriculture.

In Australia, already the world's driest continent, salinity had become a major threat to a large proportion of key farming areas, while in the United States wide areas were using substantially more water than could be naturally replenished.

Even in Japan with its high rainfall, contamination of water supplies had become a serious issue.

The overall picture would only get worse in coming years as global warming brought lower rainfall and increased evaporation of water and changed the pattern of snow melting from mountain areas.

Here are seven ways to tackle the problem:

- conserving catchments and wetlands;
- balancing conservation and consumption;

- changing attitudes to water;
- repairing ageing infrastructure;
- increase charges to farmers for water use;
- reduce water contamination and;
- more study of water systems.

## Combating climate change and preserving biodiversity

If it is possible to move towards a global system in which there is sustained action on issues of the socio-economic divide and environmental constraints, then it would be possible to envisage a genuine easing of the tensions that are currently developing in an increasingly fractured world. They would need to be accompanied by a wide range of measures intended to curb excesses of militarisation and weapons development, as well as international cooperation on issues of conflict prevention, peace-keeping and post-conflict peace-building.[28]

The ongoing decline in genetic diversity inevitably diminishes food security. One critical aim of the International Treaty is to conserve the remaining genetic diversity of cultivated plants, and to ensure that it is available to farmers and crop breeders worldwide.

The Convention on Biological Diversity is one of the most broadly subscribed international environmental treaties in the world. Opened for signature at the Earth Summit in Rio de Janeiro Brazil in 1992, it currently has 188 Parties – 187 States and the European Community – who have committed themselves to its three main goals: the conservation of biodiversity, sustainable use of its components and

---

[28] P. Rogers "The United Nations and the Promotion of Peace," in V. Mehta (2005), *The United Nations and its Future in the 21^{st} Century.* Nottingham: Spokesman

the equitable sharing of the benefits arising out of the utilisation of genetic resources.

A major contribution to achieving the three objectives of the Convention and the 2010 biodiversity target, as well as the United Nation's MDGs will be a historic achievement. For the climate change programme to succeed, let us remember the words of the UN Secretary-General, Kofi Annan, who at the ratification of the Kyoto Protocol by the Russian Federation, said:

> "This is a historic step forward in the world's efforts to combat a truly global threat. Most important, it ends a long period of uncertainty…. Those countries that have ratified the Protocol, and which have been trying to reduce emissions of greenhouse gases even before its entry into force, now have a legally binding obligation to do so. Businesses that have been exploring the realm of green technology now have a strong signal about the market viability of their products and services. And the financial community and insurance industry, which have been trying to 'put a price' on the risks associated with climate change, now have a stronger basis for their decision making on incentives and corporate performance."[29]

[29] UNEP News Centre, "Russia's Ratification of the Kyoto Climate Treaty 'Historic' says Kofi Annan," 18 November 2004
http://www.unep.org/Documents.Multilingual/Default.asp?DocumentID=412&ArticleID=4668&l=en

**5**

# Diseases – The Silent Killers – HIV/AIDS, Malaria and Cancer

*Can the onslaught of deadly diseases be halted?*

### Introduction

Poverty, lack of access to health care, antibiotic resistance, migration and changing environmental and development activities all contribute to the expanding impact of infectious diseases. More than 90 percent of the deaths from infectious diseases worldwide are caused by only a handful of diseases. Respiratory infections, HIV/AIDS, diarrhoeal diseases, tuberculosis, malaria and measles are also the leading cause of death in sub-Saharan Africa. Whilst other less studied infectious diseases cause chronic disability and stigma for millions.

The HIV/AIDS pandemic now kills more than 3 million people each year and poses an unprecedented threat to human development and security. The disease is ravaging millions of families and tens of millions of orphans. The number of women affected by it is one and a half times greater than that of men. Women currently account for 40% of the new cases for this disease as opposed to 10%, 10 years ago. AIDS affects a quarter of the adult population in some countries.

In the 25 years since it was first reported, AIDS has become the leading cause of premature deaths in sub-Sahara Africa (where two-thirds of all carriers of the HIV virus are to be found) and the fourth largest killer worldwide. More than 20 million people have died around the world since the epidemic began, and by 2004, an estimated 40 million people were living with HIV. In addition to the incalculable human suffering that AIDS has brought, the epidemic has reversed decades of development progress in the worst-affected countries. Almost no country has escaped its wrath.

Global spread of malaria, at the end of 2004, reached 107 countries and territories. Some 3.2 billion people lived in areas at risk of malaria transmission. An estimated 350–500 million clinical malaria episodes occur annually. Worldwide spread of malaria is likely to be one of the more dangerous consequences of global warming unless a truly efficient vaccine is found for that disease. Ten million children die every year of preventable diseases.

According to the World Health Organization (WHO), some 30 million deaths every year are thought to be attributable to water pollution, in the form of cholera, various types of hepatitis, dengue fever, malaria, and other parasitic diseases.

It is estimated that 4 million children die every year from illnesses transmitted by water unfit for drinking, that is, one child in every eight seconds. Eight million people are likely to die by 2020 of diseases transmitted by mosquitoes and on account of water contamination.

More than one in three people will be diagnosed with a type of cancer during their lifetime (about one out of every two men and one out of every three women), and one in four will die from cancer. According to the American Cancer Society (ACS), cancer is the second leading cause of death in the US. Almost every family has experienced the tragedy of contracting this cruel disease. It is important to realise that cancer is not a single disease with a single type of treatment. There are more than 200 different kinds of cancer that can occur anywhere in the body, each with its own name and treatment.


## HIV and AIDS

The world has reached a crucial moment in the history of HIV/AIDS, and now has an unprecedented opportunity to alter its course. The most important message of the World Health Report[30] is that, today, the international community has the chance to change the history of health for generations to come and open the door to better health for all. Tackling the disease is the world's most urgent public health challenge. Unknown barely a quarter of a century ago, it is now the leading cause of death for young adults worldwide.

We are living in a time of unprecedented opportunities for health. In spite of many difficulties, technology has made important advances and international investment in health has, at last, begun to flow. Most of the increased funding is for the fight against the virus. It brings a welcome and long overdue improvement in the prospects for controlling the worst global epidemic in several centuries. The responsibility of WHO and its partners in this effort is to ensure that the increased funding is used in such a way as to enable countries to fight the disease, and at the same time strengthen their health systems.

Future generations will judge our era, in a large part, by our response to the AIDS pandemic. By tackling it decisively we will also be building health systems that can meet the health needs of today and tomorrow, and continue the advance to Health for All. This is an opportunity we cannot afford to miss.

---

[30] World Health Organisation (2004), "The World Health Report," Geneva. http://www.who.int/whr/en/

# Vijay Mehta

Effectively tackling the virus is the world's most urgent public health challenge. Unknown a quarter of a century ago, the pandemic is now the leading cause of death and lost years of productive life for adults aged 15–59 years worldwide.

A comprehensive strategy links prevention, treatment, care and support for people living with the virus. Until now, treatment has been the most neglected element in most developing countries. Yet among all possible HIV-related interventions it is treatment that can most effectively drive health systems strengthening, enabling poor countries to protect their people from a wide range of health threats. This report shows how international organisations, national governments, the private sector and communities can combine their strengths to expand access to its treatment, reinforce HIV prevention and strengthen health systems in some of the countries where they are currently weakest, for the long-term benefit of all.

Almost 6 million people in developing countries will die in the near future if they do not receive treatment – but only about 400,000 of them were receiving it in 2003. In September 2003, WHO, the Joint United Nations Programme on UNAIDS and the Global Fund declared lack of access to AIDS treatment with antiretroviral medicines, a global health emergency. In response, these organisations and their partners launched an effort to provide 3 million people in developing countries with antiretroviral therapy by the end of 2005 – the 3 by 5 initiative – one of the most ambitious public health projects ever conceived. This is a crucial moment in the history of the virus, and an unprecedented opportunity to alter its course.

Treatment is the key to change. It is now possible to save the lives of millions of people who need that treatment but do not yet have access to it. Almost 6 million people now need antiretroviral drugs but only about 400,000 received them in 2003. This knowledge underpins the commitment of WHO and its partners to help provide 3 million people in developing countries with antiretroviral therapy by the end of 2005 – and not to stop there.

The treatment expansion initiative far outreaches the capacities of any single organisation. It is one of the most ambitious public health projects in history, and is fraught with difficulties. But within the multiple partnerships of the international community, the knowledge that this *can* be done is leading to the recognition that it *must* be done.

The moral imperative needs no reinforcement, yet there are other excellent reasons to support the treatment initiative. As WHO report has shown, the long-term economic and social costs of the disease in many countries have been seriously underestimated, and some countries in sub-Saharan Africa may be brought to the brink of economic collapse. Treatment expansion is vital to protect their stability and security and to strengthen the foundations of their future development. Furthermore, and of inestimable importance, treatment can be the accelerator that drives efforts to strengthen health systems in all developing countries.

Building up health systems is essential, not just in the fight against the virus but also in generally improving access to better health care for those most in need. This report has demonstrated how international organisations, national governments, the private sector and communities can combine their strengths to achieve this objective.

Advocacy by WHO and its partners for increased international investment in health is beginning to bear fruit. Countries should get the maximum public health benefit from new funds that are now becoming available. Although largely intended for the virus, these resources can simultaneously strengthen some of the world's most fragile health systems.

Beyond 2005 lies the challenge of extending treatment to many more millions of people, and of maintaining it for the rest of their lives, while simultaneously building and sustaining the health infrastructures to make that huge task possible. The success of this action cannot be guaranteed. But inaction will not be forgiven. It will be judged by those who suffer and die needlessly today, and by the historians of tomorrow. They will have a right to ask why, if we let the chance of changing history slip through our fingers, we did not act in time.

## Responses to diseases in the past – slow and shocking

At least 1.3 billion people worldwide lack access to the most basic healthcare, often because there is no health worker. The shortage is global, but the burden is greatest in countries overwhelmed by poverty and disease where these health workers are needed most. Shortages are most severe in sub-Saharan Africa, which has 11% of the world's population and 24% of the global burden of disease but only 3% of the world's health workers.

Over the past three decades, the world has seen the emergence of new infectious diseases, a resurgence of older diseases and a spread of resistance to a growing number of mainstay antibiotic drugs. Recent outbreaks of polio threaten to undermine its near eradication, which was one of the great accomplishments of the twentieth century. These trends signify a dramatic decay in local and global public health capacity.

International response to the epidemic was shockingly slow and remains shamefully ill-resourced. The first major international initiative on was started by the Global Programme on AIDS, came only in 1987, 6 years after the first cases of HIV were identified and after it had infected millions of people worldwide. Nine years and 25 million infections later, the Joint UN Programme on UNAIDS was created to coordinate UN agencies.

By 2000, when the Security Council first discussed the virus as a threat to international peace and security, the number of deaths per year from the pandemic in Africa had outstripped the number of battle deaths in all the civil wars fought in the 1990s. By 2003, when the Global Fund to Fight AIDS, Tuberculosis and Malaria (GFATM) was created, there were more than 11 million children orphaned by HIV/AIDS in Africa.

Despite major international initiatives, the spread of the disease is still rampant. In the most affected countries of sub-Saharan Africa, the impact of the pandemic is becoming more acute. In Asia, the number of infections exceeds 7 million and is increasing rapidly. Although international resources devoted to meeting the challenge of the virus have increased from about $250 million in 1996 to about $2.8 billion in 2002, more than $10 billion annually is needed to stem the pandemic.

The experience of some countries shows that properly funded and institutionalised efforts can yield remarkable successes in the fight against the pandemic. By contrast, where Governments have refused to acknowledge the gravity of the threat and failed to address the problem, countries have experienced a dramatic turn for the worse and international efforts to address the problem have been hampered. Leaders of affected countries need to mobilise resources, commit funds and engage civil society and the private sector in disease-control efforts.

The fight against HIV/AIDS, tuberculosis and malaria depends on capable, responsible States with functioning public health systems.

# Vijay Mehta

The absence of health facilities is the primary factor spurring the proliferation of malaria. Funding gaps are preventing health sector reforms in many heavily burdened countries, particularly those in South Asia and sub-Saharan Africa. Inconsistent or partial treatment, resulting from insufficient funding, has allowed new strains of tuberculosis to develop that are far more difficult to treat. Even when programme funding for the pandemic is available, inadequate or non-existent health facilities in the poorest areas of sub-Saharan Africa hinder programmes from being effectively or sustainably implemented. International donors, in partnership with national authorities and local civil society organisations, should undertake a major new global initiative to rebuild local and national public health systems throughout the developing world.

## Malaria and the UN's decade to roll back malaria 2001-2010

The World Malaria Report 2005 reviews each of the three world regions that are significantly affected by malaria and shows wide variation in the grip of the disease. What is clear is that there is no simple correlation between the proportion of each region's population that is considered at risk and the numbers who fall ill or die. Over 80% of malaria deaths occur in Africa where around 66% of the population are thought to be at risk. In contrast, less than 15% of the global total of malaria deaths occurs in Asia (including Eastern Europe), despite the fact that an estimated 49% of the people in this region are living under threat from the disease. In the Americas, 14% of the population are at risk, but the region sees only a tiny fraction of global malaria-related deaths.

As these figures make clear, malaria exacts its heaviest toll on the African continent. Chiefly, there are two explanations. First, the climate and ecology of tropical Africa provide ideal conditions for *Anopheles gambiae* – the most efficient of the mosquitoes carrying the malaria parasite – to thrive. And it is here also that *Plasmodium falciparum* – the most deadly species of the malaria parasite – is most common. This fatal combination greatly increases the transmission of malaria infection and the risk of disease and death. Second, poverty and lack of good-quality health care have hindered the control and treatment efforts that have had a significant impact elsewhere in the world.

Malaria is a problem to which answers are available. The know-how, the plans, and the technologies are all in place; nd they are beginning to work. Just two things stand in the way of taking treatment and prevention measures to scale: a shortage of funds and a shortage of in-country capacity to put plans into action on the ground. This is the decade to take action: the time is now.

WHO estimates that around US 3.2 billion each year is required to finance effective malaria control worldwide. Governments in malaria-affected countries are committed to increasing their own resources for malaria control, and multilateral and bilateral donors have helped to provide extra money. The Global Fund to Fight AIDS, Tuberculosis and Malaria (GFATM) is also an important international funding source. But still, the funds available fall far short of what is needed.

In the words of Professor Jeffrey Sachs, Director of the Earth Institute at Columbia University and Special Advisor to United Nations Secretary-General Kofi Annan,

"Comprehensive malaria control is the lowest-hanging fruit on the planet. For just US\$ 3 per person per year in the rich countries, it is possible to fund the comprehensive control of malaria in Africa, ensuring universal access to life-saving nets, effective medicines, and other control measures. Millions of lives in the coming years can be saved, with profound economic benefits as well. This is an historic bargain too great to miss."

## Cancer and actions which can make a difference

The World Cancer Report, produced by the WHO, states that global cancer rates could increase by 50% to 15 million by 2020.[31] It also provides clear evidence that action on smoking, diet and infections can prevent one-third of cancers; another third can be cured.

In the year 2000, malignant tumours were responsible for 12 per cent of the nearly 56 million deaths worldwide from all causes. In many countries, more than a quarter of deaths are attributable to cancer. In 2000, 5.3 million men and 4.7 million women developed a malignant tumour and altogether 6.2 million died from the disease. The report also reveals that cancer has emerged as a major public health problem in developing countries, matching its effect in industrialised nations.

> "The World Cancer Report tells us that cancer rates are set to increase at an alarming rate globally. We can make a difference by taking action today. We have the opportunity to stem this increase. This report calls on Governments, health practitioners and the general public to take urgent action. Action now can prevent one third of cancers, cure another third, and provide good, palliative care to the remaining third who need it", said Dr. Paul Kleihues, Director of the International Agency for Research on Cancer (IARC) and co-editor of the World Cancer Report.

---

[31] World Health Organisation (2003), "The World Cancer Report", Geneva. http://www.who.int/cancer/publications/en/

# Fortune Forum Code

In 2020, regions with traditionally low numbers of cancer deaths could see alarming increases in mortality rates. Regions including Northern Africa and Western Asia, South America, the Caribbean, and South East Asia could face sharp increases of over 75% in the number of cancer deaths in 2020 as compared to 2000.

Examples of areas where action can make a difference to stemming the increase of cancer rates and preventing a third of cases are:

- Reduction of tobacco consumption. It remains the most important avoidable cancer risk. In the 20th century, approximately 100 million people died world-wide from tobacco-associated diseases.

- Early detection through screening, particularly for cervical and breast cancers, allow for prevention and successful cure.

## The crisis in human resources and why the workforce is important

A serious shortage of health workers in 57 countries is impairing provision of essential, life-saving interventions such as childhood immunisation, safe pregnancy and delivery services for mothers, and access to treatment for HIV/AIDS, malaria and tuberculosis. This shortage, combined with a lack of training and knowledge, is also a major obstacle for health systems as they attempt to respond effectively to chronic diseases, avian influenza and other health challenges, according to The World Health Report 2006 – Working together for health.[32]

---

[32] WHO media centre, "World Health Report outlines need for more investment in health workforce to improve working conditions, revitalise training institutions and anticipate future challenges," 7 April 2006
See World Health Organisation (2006), "The World Health Report," Geneva.

# Vijay Mehta

More than 4 million additional doctors, nurses, midwives, managers and public health workers are urgently needed to fill the gap in these 57 countries, 36 of which are in sub-Saharan Africa, says the Report, which is highlighted by events in many cities around the world to mark World Health Day. Every country needs to improve the way it plans for, educates and employs the doctors, nurses and support staff who make up the health workforce and provide them with better working conditions.

In this first decade of the 21st century, immense advances in human well-being coexist with extreme deprivation. In global health we are witnessing the benefits of new medicines and technologies. But there are unprecedented reversals. Life expectancies have collapsed in some of the poorest countries to half the level of the richest – attributable to the ravages of HIV/AIDS in parts of sub-Saharan Africa and to more than a dozen "failed states". These setbacks have been accompanied by growing fears, in rich and poor countries alike, of new infectious threats such as SARS and avian influenza and "hidden" behavioural conditions such as mental disorders and domestic violence.

The world community has sufficient financial resources and technologies to tackle most of these health challenges; yet today many national health systems are weak, unresponsive, inequitable – even unsafe. What is needed now is political will to implement national plans, together with international cooperation to align resources, harness knowledge and build robust health systems for treating and preventing disease and promoting population health. Developing capable, motivated and supported health workers is essential for overcoming bottlenecks to achieve national and global health goals. Health care is a labour-intensive service industry. Health service providers are the personification of a system's core

http://www.who.int/whr/en/

# Fortune Forum Code

values – they heal and care for people, ease pain and suffering, prevent disease and mitigate risk – the human link that connects knowledge to health action.

At the heart of each and every health system, the workforce is central to advancing health. There is ample evidence that worker numbers and quality are positively associated with immunisation coverage, outreach of primary care, and infant, child and maternal survival. The quality of doctors and the density of their distribution have been shown to correlate with positive outcomes in cardiovascular diseases. Conversely, child malnutrition has worsened with staff cutbacks during health sector reform. Cutting-edge quality improvements of health care are best initiated by workers themselves because they are in the unique position of identifying opportunities for innovation. In health systems, workers function as gatekeepers and navigators for the effective, or wasteful, application of all other resources such as drugs, vaccines and supplies.

These challenges, past and future, are well illustrated by considering how the workforce must be mobilised to address specific health challenges.

- The MDGs target the major poverty-linked diseases devastating poor populations, focusing on maternal and child health care and the control of HIV/AIDS, tuberculosis and malaria. Countries that are experiencing the greatest difficulties in meeting the MDGs, many in sub-Saharan Africa, face absolute shortfalls in their health workforce. Major challenges exist in bringing priority disease programmes into line with primary care provision, deploying workers equitably for universal access to HIV/AIDS treatment, scaling up delegation to community workers, and creating public health strategies for disease prevention.

- Chronic diseases, consisting of cardiovascular and metabolic diseases, cancers, injuries, and neurological and psychological disorders, are major burdens affecting rich and poor populations alike. New paradigms of care are driving a shift from acute tertiary hospital care to patient-centred, home-based and team-driven care requiring new skills, disciplinary collaboration and continuity of care – as demonstrated by innovative approaches in Europe and North America. Risk reduction, moreover, depends on measures to protect the environment and the modification of lifestyle factors such as diet, smoking and exercise through behaviour change.

- Health crises of epidemics, natural disasters and conflict are sudden, often unexpected, but invariably recurring. Meeting the challenges requires coordinated planning based on sound information, rapid mobilisation of workers, command-and-control responses, and intersectoral collaboration with nongovernmental organisations, the military, peacekeepers and the media. Specialised workforce capacities are needed for the surveillance of epidemics or for the reconstruction of societies torn apart by ethnic conflict. The quality of response ultimately depends upon workforce preparedness based on local capacity backed by timely international support.

These examples illustrate the enormous richness and diversity of the workforce needed to tackle specific health problems. The tasks and functions required are extraordinarily demanding, and each must be integrated into coherent national health systems. All of the problems necessitate efforts beyond the health sector. Effective strategies therefore require all relevant actors and organisations to work together.

## Moving forward together

Moving forward on the plan of action necessitates that stakeholders work together through inclusive alliances and networks – local, national and global – across health problems, professions, disciplines, ministries, sectors and countries. Cooperative structures can pool limited talent and fiscal resources and promote mutual learning. Figure 5 proposes how a global workforce alliance can be launched to bring relevant stakeholders to accelerate core country programmes.

A premier challenge is advocacy that promotes workforce issues to a high place on the political agenda and keeps them there. The moment is ripe for political support as problem awareness is expanding, effective solutions are emerging, and various countries are already pioneering interventions. Workforce development is a continuous process that is always open for improvement. However, immediate acceleration of performance can be attained in virtually all countries if well-documented solutions are applied. Some of the work should be implemented immediately; other aspects will take time. There are no short cuts and there is no time to lose. Now is the time for action, to invest in the future, and to advance health – rapidly and equitably.

In order to achieve the goal of getting, "the right workers with the right skills in the right place doing the right things," countries should develop plans that include the following:

- Acting now for workforce productivity: better working conditions for health workers, improved safety, better access to treatment and care;

- Anticipating what lies ahead: a well-developed plan to train the health workforce of the future;

- Acquiring critical capacity: workforce planning; development of leadership and management; standard setting, accreditation and licensing as drivers for quality improvement.

Beyond the national strategies we need global cooperation for:

- Joint investment in research and information systems;

- Agreements on ethical recruitment of and working conditions for migrant health workers and international planning on the health workforce for humanitarian emergencies or global health threats such as an influenza pandemic;

- Commitment from donor countries to assist crisis countries with their efforts to improve and support the health workforce.


**The problem with antibiotics**

The development of antibiotics in the second half of the 20th century, and successful global effort against infectious diseases, which had reached its peak with the eradication of smallpox, created the illusion that infectious diseases were being relegated into the past. But this proved to be wishful thinking. Contagious diseases have returned, threatening the lives, health, and advance of millions of people in all parts of the world. Suffice it to say that TB, which seemed to be left forever in the 19th century, in the novels of Dumas and Remarque, is killing up to 2 million every year at a rate of 4 people per minute! New diseases like HIV, have emerged. AIDS, caused by this virus, has taken a toll of more than 25 million people since 1981. Another 40 million are sentenced to death without adequate treatment.

# Fortune Forum Code

Infectious diseases have become a break on economic progress. In many African countries, it has ground to a halt, and has even been reversed by HIV. East European and Asian countries, which were gripped by the epidemic much later, may be in for similar problems. The influenza has not yet become a pandemic, but is already causing heavy economic damage by upsetting international commerce and tourism.

## A global strategy for controlling diseases

- Consolidation of global network on monitoring and controlling infectious diseases

Timely identification of emerging epidemics and an ability to predict ways of their dissemination are crucial for an adequate reply of the health system. In this context, it is important to achieve better coordination of national services (for instance, by urgently adopting international medical and sanitary rules), exchange understandable information, and enhance the potential of epidemiological services in the developing nations on timely identification and response to outbreaks of infectious diseases. It is very important to develop a system, which would help predict the ways of disease dissemination based on the information on the number of cases among humans and animals, and prevailing trends.

- Countering avian influenza and preparing for influenza pandemic

Remaining mostly an avian disease, the H5N1 influenza strain has already done heavy damage to mankind by killing people and affecting many more with the economic aftermath of the poultry epidemic. The beginning of the influenza pandemic is the worst-case scenario. It may happen if the virus develops an ability to infect humans. A influenza pandemic may have grave consequences. It is enough to recall that in 1918-1919 the Spanish influenza killed more people than World War I.

The WHO is calling upon all nations to closely follow the development of the avian influenza epidemic, and, in case of man-to-man transmission, take every effort to contain its spread. By way of preparing to a potential epidemic, it is necessary to intensify information exchange at the expert level, to explain to the public the facts about the disease; enhance the lab potential in high-risk areas; facilitate the development of national monitoring systems in close cooperation with the World Organization for Animal Health and the UN Food and Agriculture Organization (FAO); build up reserves of medicines affecting the virus, and develop vaccines for nipping in the bud the pandemic-causing virus.

The economic consequences of panic may be as dangerous as the virus itself. It is important to reduce the negative effect of a potential influenza pandemic on international trade and economic cooperation.

- Fighting HIV/AIDS

G8 sessions have often focused on fighting these leading killers. The previous commitments in this sphere, and the focus on countering them, calls for continued efforts to develop the vaccine against HIV, and enhance regional cooperation in Eastern Europe and Central Asia. It is necessary to establish a broad coalition of the civil society and commercial structures for fighting the epidemic, and taking adequate preventive measures. It is important to acknowledge the fact that the anti-HIV/AIDS effort should be multi-faceted, and should concentrate on backing the development of healthcare systems, which would be capable of carrying out preventive and treatment programs.

# Fortune Forum Code

Other efforts to control the virus is to keep it visible on the political agenda, maintaining full and unbroken funding for universal access to treatment, scientific innovation in development microbicides, and vaccines. We also need to make headway in addressing the drivers of this epidemic, especially the low status of women, homophobia, HIV-related stigma, poverty and inequality.

Follow one of the widely practiced approaches to prevention, that is, the ABC programme, for Abstain, Be faithful, and use Condoms. This approach has saved many lives and we should expand it.

- Eradication of poliomyelitis

Mankind is made some progress in the drive against infectious diseases. It has almost completely eradicated poliomyelitis, which killed and incapacitated children in the 1940s and 1950s. Individual cases occur in few countries, but inoculation programmes will soon eliminate them for good. It is necessary to find the funds for a final attack against poliomyelitis.

Victory is around the corner, and the experts are already discussing the use of the volunteers and organisations, involved in fighting poliomyelitis, for the struggle against other infections.

- Measles and other preventable diseases

Although there exists an effective and safe vaccine against measles, it continues killing thousands of children all over the world. Mankind has the vaccine which could save children, and wipe out measles for good. It is necessary to deliver it to those areas, which are in need of it. G8 nations support the initiatives of the Global Alliance for Vaccines and Immunization, and urging the WHO to start implementing its plans on preventing and eradicating measles.

Focus also needs to be on so-called forgotten diseases - different infections, which are causing suffering and death in the tropic regions, but which enjoy much less attention. In addition, it is important to concentrate on the resistance of viruses to medicines and on the need for global cooperation to resolve this problem.

- Access to treatment and prevention

Finances and personnel are essential for planning the fight against infectious diseases. Limited potentialities of the healthcare systems are a major barrier to prevention and treatment of infectious diseases. It is therefore essential to build them up, and primarily, to enroll professionals in the effort. The WHO should find ways of achieving this goal, which must be supported by donor organisations.

Improving healthcare staff resources and treating patients requires financing. In this respect, different innovation financial mechanisms could be of use, as they could find money to implement programs fighting infectious diseases.

- Prevention and struggle against epidemics caused by natural calamities and technological disasters

Tsunamis in Asia, hurricanes in America, and earthquakes in South Asia have demonstrated the importance of fast and coordinated response to natural calamities. History shows that the destruction of the healthcare infrastructure, which is often a result of major natural and technological disasters, makes the onslaught of infectious diseases much more likely. Therefore, it is necessary to boost the ability of the developing nations to cope with the aftermath of disasters, and to coordinate the use of the available resources.

A set of important anti-infection priorities are as follows:

# Fortune Forum Code

- promotion of institutional health care development;

- support for medicine and vaccine research and production;

- support for equal access to diagnostic, prevention, and treatment facilities;

- support for global programs fighting infectious diseases;

- promotion of intranational cooperation – notably between public, private, and civic institutions – to fight infectious diseases.

Unfortunately, for all the efforts made and planned, the international community is still far from the point where infectious diseases are controllable and no longer pose a threat to the progress of mankind, and where every country can give its citizens access to the diagnostics, prevention, and treatment of diseases.

Vijay Mehta

# 6

# Education For All

*Can it bring peace and harmony to the world?*

## Introduction

Why education, especially peace education is an extremely important global issue? What is peace education and what are its goals, scope and purpose? What is a culture of peace and what form of action can we take at schools, home and in our communities to advance peace and development? And what are the obstacles, opportunities and contribution we can make to modern education?[33]

Universal primary education and getting rid of illiteracy is one of the eight Millennium Development Goals (MDGs)[34], to be achieved by 2015. However the reality is that one in six adults on the planet cannot read or write. Some 600 million women and 300 million men remain illiterate around the world. Some 115 million children between six and eleven –one in five – are not in school. Of those who go to school, one in four drop out before completing 5 years of basic education. South Asia, Africa, and the Middle East are the 3 regions where these problems are most severe. Many children in developed and developing countries have been deprived of their education

---

[33] This is part of an extract of an earlier speech by Vijay Mehta – "Peace belongs to us all: Establishing peace through teaching peace," 19 June 2006, Houses of Parliament, UK. **www.vmpeace.org**

[34] 1. Eradicate extreme poverty and hunger by half, 2. Achieve universal primary education, 3. Promote gender equality and empower women, 4. Reduce child mortality, 5. Improve maternal health, 6. Combat HIV/AIDS, malaria and other diseases, 7. Ensure environmental sustainability, and 8. Develop a global partnership for development.

# Fortune Forum Code

owing to child labour and poverty.

India has approximately 350 million people who cannot read or write, the United Nations Children's Fund has said that it is the most illiterate country in the world. The image of 350 million people being unable to read and write isn't just frightening; it's daunting.

Moreover, throughout the developing world, the quality of primary, secondary and university education is rarely up to the standards required by the new world economy. And globally, we are far away from seeing the emergence of a badly needed system of international accreditation.

## Why education is an extremely important global issue

- *Education is key for an ethical foundation of our society and to protect core values of life.* These shared values comprise some of the most basic aspirations of human kind – freedom, equality, solidarity, tolerance, respect for nature, shared responsibility and multiculturalism.

- *Education is central to the construction of genuinely democratic societies including good governance and the rule of law.* Even from a moral standpoint, one could argue that education is a kind of universal right because it provides "human capabilities," to make choices, and steer towards a better life.

- *Education is key to building the sense of global citizenship that global problem-solving requires.* And it is a major tool for developing a sense of shared global values that may help bring harmony between civilisations and cultures.

- *Education is the most powerful instrument for reducing poverty and inequality* and for laying the basis for sustainable growth. It

87

has strong links, not just to productivity growth, but to improve health, to the ability to understand the need to care for the natural environment, and even to the growth of population.

- *Environmental education is important for countering the effects of climate change, for turning our back on oil, gas and coal and for finding alternative sources of energy.*

- *The new world economy, with its knowledge intensity, requires a leap forward in each country's education effort* – from primary to higher education, and even to lifelong learning and the accreditation of competencies. If that does not happen in a very large number of countries, we should expect even greater inequalities between countries over the decades to come.

- *We need universal education to tackle global issues of wars, terrorism, poverty and climate change.* Lack of peace education is the primary reason for conflicts, terrorism and mayhem around the world. Global security and environmental crises are both pressing problems of our age, yet poverty is the most defining challenge of this century, hence the need for education.

- *Education is necessary for the advancement of science, culture and civilisation for all of us to share a common vision of humanity.* It is vital to have craving for knowledge and a global quest for excellence and critical thinking which can only come from ideas generated by reading books and education. People cannot have this opportunity to realise this dream if they are unable to read and write. Total literacy requires commitment, sacrifice and a huge amount of goodwill.

- *Education is development. It creates choices and opportunities for people,* reduces the twin burdens of poverty and diseases, and gives a stronger voice in society. For nations, it creates a dynamic workforce and well-informed citizens able to compete and cooperate globally – opening doors to economic and social prosperity.

- *Education is essential for media coverage for shaping the events in war and peace.* It challenges the one-dimensional war reporting offering concrete alternatives rather than mere criticism and maps a conflict rather as a roundtable consisting of many parties, many issues offering concrete alternatives rather than mere (if solid) criticism. The major thesis is that the present way of reporting war leaves out the most important part of the story: how a conflict might be transcended.

## What is peace education? What are its goals, scope and purpose?

Peace education is a global vision, a long-term way of investing in the education of our youth and adults as future peace makers, responsible citizens and democratic leaders. Education enriches knowledge of world affairs, conflict resolution and the global economy. It helps to build today's youth to become tomorrows global ambassadors and business leaders.

Peace education embodies the very essence of education, its methods, principles and overwhelming potential, so that we may offer and nurture within all our children and adults those attitudes, values and skills that are conducive to living in harmony with others, respecting their human rights, resolving conflicts non-violently and building understanding and solidarity with those who are different in culture, religion or language.

Peace Education believes in the critical role of transforming cultures of violence and war into cultures of peace worldwide; where being different is being unique and the concept of world citizenship is celebrated.

There are parallels in Gandhi's view on education and J. Dewey's work in America. Both of them advocate that a goal of education is a preparation for real life and the education of the heart. As such, the personal and moral growth, leading to a non-violent approach to life, is the key goal. The work we are undertaking today for conflict resolution and mediation under peace studies would have been approved by both of them.

Recent decades have witnessed increased interest in peace education address global problems. It inquires into whether problems of violence, war, and injustice at all levels, from the local to the global, have been devised. Thus, a range of multicultural education, gender education, environmental education, development education, interfaith education, education for human rights, education for values, conflict resolution, and non-violence are now available to peace educators.

It is increasingly maintained that peace education should provide opportunities for realistic and informed appraisal of these global problems, emphasising positive alternatives and multiple possibilities for problem resolution to balance the many negative images of an inevitable global disaster, to which the young and adults are exposed on a daily basis. To achieve the balance, there is a need for the development of critical inquiry and problem solving skills and for the nurturing of creative imagination to envision alternatives.

An alternative peaceful future is defined, not only as the absence of open hostilities, or negative peace, but as the presence of peacemaking processes and conditions likely to ensure a secure, durable, positive peace. It implies a state of wellbeing, a dynamic social progress in which justice, equity, and respect for basic human rights are maximised, and violence, both physical and structural, is minimised. Comprehensive peace education is rooted in this holistic, dynamic view of peace and is explicitly value-based. Two core values of comprehensive peace education are non-violence and social justice. These values underline and are defined through all process of peace learning. A value such as non-violence is manifested through other values such as respect for human rights, freedom, and trust, while social justice is realised by values such as equality, responsibility and solidarity.

The deepest purpose of all education should be the promotion of the world characterised by peace, that is, cooperation and fraternity, where conflicts are managed constructively and non-violently. Education is a key element in the fight against poverty and ignorance.

## Culture of peace

The culture of peace consists of values, attitudes and behaviours that reject violence. In a peaceful world, we solve problems through dialogue and negotiations.

Culture of peace is a stage where differences of two conflicting individuals or states melt into a relationship of peace, harmony, co-operation, love and understanding. When you reach that level, no one is ever at war with anyone else, and the need for peace education becomes obsolete.

However, we are living in a world of wars, conflict, hatred and fear. The last century was the most violence-ridden century in the history of mankind. In the name of country, ethnicity, religion or belief, people were harmed only because they appeared to be different – neighbours harmed neighbours, women were dishonoured and children were robbed of their future.

# Vijay Mehta

To me culture of peace is a set of values, attitudes and ways of life based on the principle of freedom, justice, democracy, tolerance, solidarity, and respect for diversity, dialogue and understanding which will bring about the transformation from a culture of war to a culture of peace.

For the success of our message, we need a grand alliance for a culture of peace. Civil society has a very important and definite role in that alliance. Without its proactive role, we can never involve communities and societies in the building of a global culture of peace.

Teachers and students should teach and learn and spread the virtues of peace. All of us need to join the global movement for a culture of peace and make a contribution toward peace. And please remember, there are no small contributions for peace. They all add up.

*Non-violence is the cornerstone in building a culture of peace. The core values of non-violence – respect for life, and the pursuit of justice and dignity for all humanity –* reflect key values from the world's main spiritual traditions. For some people, non-violence is a set of values that bears witness to their religious beliefs. These values are shared by many people who do not identify with any particular religion. They also form the basis of important international human rights treaties.

*Non-violence is a way of life. It is also a means to make social, political and economic change.* Exploring non-violence begins with looking at power. Many people define power as the opportunity to control other people or resources. In this definition, power is assumed to be based on violence: to gain more power over people or resources means using more violence. Non-violence offers another definition of power. Non-violence seeks to empower communities and individuals. It works to help people find power within themselves, and to share power. This is power inside and power with people, not power over others.

*Non-violence assumes that power derives from cooperation.* All systems of injustice need people's cooperation to continue. A change in the power relationship can occur when cooperation is denied or withdrawn.

Examples of this took place throughout the 1980s and 1990s in Latin America, the Philippines, and Eastern Europe. In these cases, masses of non-violent and unarmed people toppled governments who used physical, psychological and economic violence in order to stay in power.

More concrete examples of spiritually based non-violence include the Christian Plowshares movement. Inspired by the Biblical passage (Micah 4:3), which states, "they will hammer their swords into plowshares". Plowshares activists enter military bases in Europe or the USA and hammer planes and other military equipment. They use the resulting court cases against them to educate the public about the suffering the arms trade creates.

In another example, Buddhist monks and nuns in Cambodia now organise dhammayatras, traditional walks from village to village in order to explain Buddhist teachings, to spread life-saving information about HIV/AIDS, land mines, and the need for peace.

## Eight action areas for peace in school, home and community

The General Assembly of the UN has designated 2001-2010 as the International Decade for a culture of peace and non-violence for the world.

*Fostering a culture of peace through education* by promoting education for all, focusing especially on girls; revising curricula to promote the qualitative values, attitudes and behaviour inherent in a culture of peace; training for conflict prevention and resolution, dialogue, consensus-building and active non-violence.

*Promoting sustainable economic and social development* by targeting the eradication of poverty; focusing on the special needs of children and women; working towards environmental sustainability; fostering national and international cooperation to reduce economic and social inequalities.

*Promoting respect for all human rights* by distributing the Universal Declaration of Human Rights at all levels and fully implementing international instruments on human rights.

*Ensuring equality between women and men* by integrating a gender perspective and promoting equality in economic, social and political decision-making; eliminating all forms of discrimination and violence against women; supporting and aiding women in crisis situations resulting from war and all other forms of violence.

*Fostering democratic participation* by educating responsible citizens; reinforcing actions to promote democratic principles and practices; establishing and strengthening national institutions and processes that promote and sustain democracy.

As part of our citizenship curriculum, we should celebrate our past successes like the Magna Carta, and other constitutional documents of our past cultural and social history. These are important for a vigorous exploration of our democratic heritage in schools and communities alike.

Magna Carta curbed the power of the monarch, safe-guarded the Church and gave ordinary people rights under common law. Although not regarded as enormously significant at the time, it set

# Fortune Forum Code

down basic ideas of liberty, democracy and constitutionalism which, after 800 years, are taken for granted.

*Advancing understanding, tolerance and solidarity* by promoting a dialogue among civilizations; actions in favour of vulnerable groups; respect for difference and cultural diversity.

Our beautiful planet is torn apart by religious dogmatism and extremism. In this respect, the role of education, especially teaching freedom of thought – compassion, forgiveness and creativity cannot be overestimated. This is what makes us different from other species.

*Supporting participatory communication and the free flow of information and knowledge* by means of such actions as support for independent media in the promotion of a culture of peace; effective use of media and mass communications; measures to address the issue of violence in the media; knowledge and information sharing through new technologies.

*Promoting international peace and security* through action such as the promotion of general and complete disarmament; greater involvement of women in prevention and resolution of conflicts and in promoting a culture of peace in post-conflict situations; initiatives in conflict situations; encouraging confidence-building measures and efforts for negotiating peaceful settlements.

In this respect, the role of media, especially peace journalism, is important. Instead of one dimensional war reporting between "goodies" or "baddies", journalists should offer concrete alternatives as a roundtable consisting of many parties, rather than mere criticism.

# Vijay Mehta

## Obstacles, barriers, opportunities and recommendations of peace education

Obstacles and barriers:

- The biggest hindrance to education and development is military spending and war-related costs. The US government spends approximately $1 million every minute on military expenditure. The recent increased military spending once again for the sixth successive year rose to the trillion dollar mark since the height of the Cold War, an average of $162 per person, with the US accounting for nearly half - 47 per cent - of the total at $455 billion and the UK at $47 billion. Nobel prize-winning economist Joseph Stiglitz has made the first bold attempt to quantify the financial side of the hidden costs of the Iraq war, coming up with a whopping price tag of over $2 trillion dollars, ten times more than pre-war estimates.

Let us note some stark facts about education and poverty and compare them with social spending:

- Almost 1 billion people are illiterate around the world.

- More than 1 billion people struggle to survive on less than a $1 a day.

- If 10% of the military expenditure were diverted yearly, then we can make poverty history forever and achieve the goal of Universal Primary Education.

- *Barriers to education for all.* If education is so valuable, to individuals and to societies, why has it been so difficult to achieve universal primary education? The opportunities for education – and the barriers to it – vary by country and locality.

# Fortune Forum Code

But there are three common barriers: poor quality, insufficient funding, and the lack of schooling for displaced children. Cultural factors and gender roles can reduce the demand for education.

- Teachers are the crux of any educational system and its quality. A study of schools in India found that in half the schools investigated, there was no teaching going on at the time that the study team visited. The reason for parents' and students' disillusionment with schooling arose, not from their economic or gender biases, but from the dismal quality of schooling. The study also cited a loss of interest in school as the most common reason boys drop out.

- Costs also matter. Providing schools, especially good quality schools, requires political will, financial resources and a solid institutional structure, whether public, private or non-governmental. When governments invest too little in education, an astonishing proportion of household expenditure must go to meet the costs of primary school. "In Sub-Saharan Africa, the costs of getting a child through primary school can represent more than a quarter of the annual income of a poor household". While parental involvement is critical, costs of this magnitude clearly subvert the right of every child to primary education.

- In emergencies, children are often denied the normalcy of education precisely when they need it most. Many children – displaced by conflict, development projects, or disasters – live in temporary communities without access to schooling. This is cause for alarm because displaced and refugee children can benefit greatly from the stable social environment that schools can provide.

# Vijay Mehta

- These are but three of the issues that need to be addressed for a global commitment to schooling. The barriers to universal basic education vary in different places. But they are not mysterious. And they are achievable.

Opportunities and recommendations:

- *To change the mindset from culture of guns to culture of peace is the foremost challenge of our age.* At every level, peace education and dialogue has to be part of life to settle disputes and renounce violence.

- *Promote lifelong education for all.* Give priority, in this regard, to adult education, particularly for women, through intensive technical and vocational training in their own language, the universalisation of basic education, and the inclusion of the excluded.

- *The best way to educate and get the message to the illiterate is through music and the visual arts.* Art should be used to encourage young and adults alike to read and write and pave the way for progress.

- *Encourage continuous training for teachers and the upgrading of their skills* in order to create an interactive context for a lifelong learning process at all levels.

- *Devise all education systems along a dual axis.* Encourage all personal initiatives of knowledge acquisition and available methods and offer everyone a basic education that is a source of personal development, cultural and ethical identity and civil responsibility. Education must both build societies and train individuals; redefined civics classes should, to that end, be given priority in the whole range of the curricula.

# Fortune Forum Code

- *Anchor local dimension in worldwide dimension* and individual dimension in collective and civic dimension: accentuate the interpersonal relations in the exchange of information, provide scope for the expressions of all local and regional specificities within the worldwide network, while preventing the creation of any hegemonic culture.

- *Devise an education system in its plurality*: plurality of methods, plurality of careers, plurality of traditional and new instruments, plurality of actors, plurality of contexts (schools, but also libraries, museums, local communities and governments, enterprises and family); plurality of time sequences (childhood learning stages, but also professional life and retirement).

- *Enrich the concept of knowledge:* moving from the idea of knowledge through accumulation to the concept of awareness of methods and objectives. Learning to learn rather than merely learning. The training of teachers who are completely familiar with the new technologies and the new requirements of society must be a priority.

- *Encourage all initiatives aiming at universal access to the new information technologies;* universal not only within countries but also between the industrialised and the developing countries, in order to reduce all forms of bipolarity. As regards education, the aim should be to establish a worldwide network of education accessible to all, without frontiers or distance of any kind.

- *Develop at national and international levels policies for building communication infrastructure,* whether traditional (libraries, audio-visual and computer equipment) or related to new technologies (multimedia, CD ROMs, connection to the interne), by placing special emphasis on disadvantaged and isolated areas and by attending the interface of this infrastructure.

- *Transform universities into centres which can provide lifelong education for all*; in accordance with Article 26.1 of the Universal Declaration of Human Rights that stipulates that, "access to higher education shall be equally accessible to all on the basic merit".

- *Grant to every individual a "training voucher"*, providing access to a number of years of education which every individual can use according to choice, career, academic experience and time-scale.

- *Host MUNGA's* (Model United Nations General Assembly) or global classrooms for students across the country or the world by internet where they can step into the shoes of UN Ambassadors to debate and resolve current international issues. It will help the youth of today to acquire critical thinking and the necessary skills to become tomorrow's global leaders.

## The social purpose of peace education

*Abolishing war, renouncing violence and establishing justice.*

The main social purposes of peace education we advocate here are the elimination of social injustice, the renunciation of violence, and the abolition of war. War and all forms of violence are interrelated, as evidenced by the culture of violence that surrounds us. War is the core institution of the present global security system, the fount from which pour the rationalisation for and habits of violence found in so many aspects of life.

The knowledge, skills and, most importantly, the values that have been at the core of peace education for the past 5 decades are those required to meet the new peace challenges and opportunities of the 21st century. These challenges and opportunities, among other concerns, require of peace education more intense and focus on the practical, political uses and skills of non-violence and on the institutional tasks involved in the abolition of war. There is a widespread belief that violence is inevitable, often necessary, but there is little knowledge of the multiple alternatives to violence. Armed conflicts abound within and between nations. War is still accepted as a legitimate means through which nations can pursue and protect their national interests. It is a legally based, if not legally controlled, institution within the nation-state system. Because nation-states tenaciously hold to the right to organise and use armed forces, others, especially those seeking to challenge or take over state power, amass arms and engage in armed conflict.

The failure of nation states to actively seek alternatives to war perpetuates a belief in its legitimacy and inevitability. War must be addressed as an institution and alternatives considered in any education, seeking to contribute to sustainable global peace. It must be recognised as a systematic problem requiring an education for systematic change.

To facilitate the systematic view of war and armed conflict, peace education seeks to develop a global perspective on the problems and an understanding that humans are a single species. Peace educators have long recognised, as fundamental to the prevention of war, the need to develop and teach the concept of global interest and to engage a sense of human identity to complement and extend the national and ethnic identities through which we form our national and international loyalties and affiliations. There are a wide range of strategies available to educators seeking to achieve these particular educational goals. What we need to develop now is an equally wide range of teaching materials and approaches to deal with the tasks of institutional change, so that all learners can understand and be politically effective in the hard work of disarmament, non-violent conflict resolution, peacemaking, and peacekeeping – all that has heretofore been left to the experts, because it is assumed to be too technical for the average citizen.

All citizens need to be educated to assess and evaluate possibilities and preferences for alternative, global security systems. Demystifying the technicalities that have obscured fundamental security issues from the general citizenry is a crucial challenge to education to abolish war. So, peace education now needs to address practical proposals for disarmament and demilitarisation. Societies can be transformed if citizens see the possibilities for transformation, and if they understand the mechanism of institutional changes upon which the transformation can be built. Enabling learners to see these possibilities and to understand these mechanisms is a primary responsibility of the field of peace education for the 21st century.

**Campaign idea**

The military budget of nations should never be bigger than the budget for health, education and development. At the moment the global military spending is $1 trillion against spending on education which stands at a mere US$ 6 billion. It should be the other way around completing the urgently needed Millennium Development Goals (MDG), including achieving universal primary education and lifting Africa and other poor countries out of absolute poverty. Only then can we have any hope and chance for a safer world and better international relations.

Martin Luther King Jr said, "a nation that continues year after year to spend more money on military defence than on programmes of social uplift is approaching spiritual doom."

# Fortune Forum Code

## A peace poem

A culture of peace will be achieved when citizens of the world understand global problems; have the skills to resolve conflicts constructively; know and live by international standards of human rights, gender and racial equality; appreciate cultural diversity; and respect the integrity of the Earth. Such learning cannot be achieved without intentional, sustained and systematic education for peace.[35]

We should celebrate our past achievements which are a result of successes of civil society brought by peace education. For example Kyoto Protocol, NPT (Nuclear Non-Proliferation Treaty), UN Charter, Geneva Conventions, UDHR (Universal Declaration of Human Rights). Other achievements are Abolition of Slavery, Freedom from Colonialism, Ending of Apartheid, Fall of Berlin Wall and Magna Carta giving rights to ordinary people and initiating ideas of liberty, democracy and law.

If we are to achieve education for all, we need to remind ourselves of a Peace Poem from Pablo Cassals, the cellist from Spain that never fails to inspire me to do more for peace:

> *"Sometimes I look around me with a feeling of*
> *complete dismay. In the confusion that afflicts the*
> *world today, I see a disrespect for the very values of*
> *life. Beauty is all around us, but how many are blind to*
> *it! They look at the wonder of this earth and*
> *seem to see nothing...*
> *And what do we teach our children? We teach them*
> *that two and two make four, and that Paris is the*

---

[35] Read 101 Peace Ideas to find inspiration for action, at www.vmpeace.org.

# Vijay Mehta

*capital of France.*
*When will we also teach them what they are? We*
*should say to each of them: Do you*
*know what you are? You are a marvel. You are unique. In all the*
*years*
*that have passed, there has never been another*
*child like you. ... Yes, you are a marvel.*
*And when you grow up, can you then harm another*
*who is, like you, a marvel? You must cherish one*
*another. You must work -- we must all work -- to*
*make the world worthy of its children."*

# 7
# Making Our Interdependent World Perform For A Sustainable Future

*Can we link the agenda of development, security and environment together?*

## Introduction

Today, we are facing the challenges of poverty, war, international terrorism, violation of human rights, environmental degradation, waste of resources; all of the threats encountered at the global level which can not be solved by nation-states.

International institutions and states have not organised themselves to address the problems of development in a coherent, integrated way; and instead continue to treat poverty, infectious disease and environmental degradation as stand – alone threats. The fragmented sectoral approaches of international institutions mirror the fragmented sectoral approaches of Governments: for example, finance ministries tend to work only with the international financial institutions, development ministers only with development programmes, ministers of agriculture only with food programmes and environment ministers only with environmental agencies. Bilateral donors correctly call for better UN coordination but show little enthusiasm for similar efforts on their own account.

Existing global economic and social governance structures are woefully inadequate for the challenges ahead. To tackle the challenges of sustainable development countries must negotiate across different sectors and issues, including foreign aid, technology, trade, financial stability and development policy. Such packages are difficult to negotiate and require high-level attention and leadership from those countries that have the largest economic impacts.

The United Nations comparative advantage in addressing economic and social threats is its unparalleled convening power, which allows it to formulate common development targets and rally the international community around a consensus for achieving them. In recent years, the World Summit on Sustainable Development held in Johannesburg, South Africa, and the International Conference on Financing for Development, held in Monterrey, Mexico, have led to global understanding and ambitious programmes for alleviating poverty, providing food security, growing economies and protecting the environment in ways that benefit future generations. The United Nations Millennium Declaration contains an ambitious but feasible set of agreed targets and benchmarks, later consolidated into the MDGs, ranging from halving extreme poverty and protecting the environment to achieving greater gender equality and halting and reversing the spread of HIV/AIDS by 2015.

In 2002, world leaders agreed at Monterrey that aid donors and aid recipients both have obligations to achieve development. The primary responsibility for economic and social development lies with Governments, which must create a conducive environment for vigorous private-sector-led growth and aid effectiveness by pursuing sound economic policies, building effective and responsible institutions and investing in public and social services that will reach all of their people. In return for substantive improvements in the policies and institutions of developing countries, donor nations agreed to renew their efforts to reduce poverty, including by reducing trade barriers, increasing development assistance and providing debt relief for highly indebted poor countries.[36]

---

[36] See UN (2005) "A more secure world: Our shared responsibility," New York.

# Fortune Forum Code

## Present day threats and challenges[37]

The threats and challenges of global governance can be categorised into areas as identified by the recent UN high-level panel report: a) dangers to human security by wars and military spending and terrorism and Weapons of Mass Destruction – nuclear, biological and chemical; b) poverty, infectious diseases, and environmental degradation (including climate change, resource depletion and population imbalances); and c) organised crime, corruption, poor governance and mass migrations.

*Dangers to human security by wars and military spending*

These dangers will continue until we tackle the underlying causes of conflict. Governments will keep spending on military hardware whether they face real or imagined security threats.

No conflict today is isolated from economic forces. The uncontrolled international arms industry and the illicit trade in natural resources thrive on instability and reward it. They also undermine the ability of civil society to hold governments accountable for their management of revenues and natural resources. After 11 September 2001 and the launch of the 'War on Terror', military spending increased dramatically, led by the US, UK, France, Russia and China. Military spending is now almost at the same levels as at the height of the Cold War.

War and all forms of violence are interrelated, as is evidenced by the culture of violence that surrounds us. War is the core institution of

---

[37] This is part of an extract of an earlier speech by Vijay Mehta – "Revitalising Global Governance and Democracy", 9 March 2006, Athens Greece. www.vmpeace.org

the present global security system which brings destruction and leads to habits of violence and conflicts found in so many aspects of life all around the world.

Conflict tears apart families and splinters communities. It increases maternal mortality and the spread of disease. It destroys social infrastructure and makes work towards a better future – such as education – almost impossible. Conflict and lawlessness encourage criminality, deter investment and prevent normal economic activity. All this deepens and entrenches poverty.

*Poverty, infectious diseases, and environmental degradation*

Poverty is a political problem because, unless it is addressed, we will face a new division of the world, the consequences of which will be even more dangerous than those of the divisions we overcame by ending the East-West confrontation. Dividing the world into islands of prosperity and vast areas of poverty and despair is more dangerous than the Cold War because the two regions cannot be fenced off from each other. Despair creates fertile ground for extremism and terrorism, to say nothing of migration flows, epidemics and new hotbeds of instability. Poverty is a political problem because it cannot be separated from the problems of democracy, human rights and fundamental freedoms.

US $2500 billion is the amount of money laundered through secret bank accounts and tax heavens every year. Maintaining global financial checks approaching $1.5 trillion worth of international financial transfers take place daily, a high percentage of which is purely speculative. This reduces governments' degree of control over their fiscal policy and can threaten the stability of major currencies. It has therefore been suggested that a tax be levied on such transfers to damp down their scale. Since the proceeds would amount to billions of dollars, the UN, with its arrears problems, and the Third World with its debt load and uncertain income, have a desperate interest.

Some other causes of poverty are unserviceable debt, underinvestment in science and technology, unjust trade rules, and lack of infrastructure and education. Just for calculation, daily allowance on subsidy for every cow in the European Union currently amount to €2.50 or US$ 3.00 which exceeds the amount of money which billions of poor people get around the world.

Infectious diseases, and environmental degradation is another cause of poverty. In 25 years since it was first reported, AIDS has become the leading cause of premature deaths in sub-Sahara Africa and the fourth largest killer worldwide. Global spread of malaria and TB are other silent killers reversing decades of development progress in worst affected areas.

The widespread environmental degradation that scars our planet as seen in melting ice caps and strong hurricanes is a global problem created by over use of land, oil, fossil fuels, and gases and threatens our natural systems and resources for our existence and development. We need to reverse the depletion of natural resources. Recent studies have shown that armed forces are the single largest polluter on earth and long-term disastrous environmental, health and social consequences of war and preparation of war are well documented. If the impact of global warming is not curbed, the future might hold an eruption of desperate all out wars for food, water and energy supplies (oil & gas).

*Organised crime, corruption, poor governance and mass migrations*

Poor governance, corruption and trans-national crime allows the diversion of resources from social development to lining the pockets of corrupt elites and increase in military spending. It is evident that higher incidence of armed conflict is found in countries with a low level of economic development and poorly run democratic institutions. It is government mismanagement and distribution problems and not global food shortages that keep millions hungry.

Inter-tribal fighting, banditry, and clashes for securing natural resources is another reason for poverty. Various studies have shown how conflicts are funded by the sale of natural resources like diamonds, oil, timber, copper, and gold. Inter-tribal fighting, banditry, and clashes for securing these resources are frequent occurrences between government, paramilitary and rebel forces. The UN Security Council have recently voted for a ban on diamonds export from the Ivory Coast to stop rebels in the war divided nation from using gems to purchase arms. The war on Iraq is an example where the invasion was not undertaken to fight terrorism or eliminate weapon of mass destruction but to safeguard vital oil resources.

Managing mass migrations of humans now move in unprecedented numbers, not simply because there are more people, but because both the need and the opportunity have grown: both "push" and "pull" forces are powerful. The UN officially recognises well over 20 million refugees forced unwillingly out of their own country. Globally, about one person in a hundred is either a refugee or "displaced", i.e. forced unwillingly to move within their country. Other mass migrations are more ambiguous, particularly the uncontrolled flows in poorer countries from country to city.

**Future outlook of the world**

Global economic balances, are shifting fast in all domains – manufacturing, trading, and financial with emerging giants China and India tilting the balance. Both of these countries are developing at an unprecedented scale and will leave behind the economies of America and any individual European country. There will be a big struggle for getting oil, water and skilled labour. As they become more wealthy and powerful, they will react differently to world events by enforcing Asian values on democracy, freedom and rule of law.

## Recommendations for effective global development

- The way forward for development is to tackle new security threats and violence, promoting disarmament and human rights, thereby building a global rule of law and order. It should also manage environmental degradation, emergencies and disasters, clash of religion and culture, and the unrestrained tide of globalisation. The implementation and completion of the MDGs should be a top priority. Most importantly the international community has the moral obligation and duty to control and intervene in countries if they are sliding into chaos, lawlessness, violence, and unable to protect its citizens from rape, murder and killings. The international community should also build on some of the successes of the summit of world leaders in New York in September 2005.

- Individuals should be empowered with unprecedented development in information and technology so that they can mould their destiny and change their lives for the better.

- We should find holistic solutions to all the interrelated issues and take responsibility to deal collectively and have a multilateral approach in dealing with threats and challenges of today. The concept of common security – peace, environment, social justice and environmental protection – reflects more accurately the purpose of the UN Charter, its treaties and conventions.

- The international community need to link the agenda of development, environment and disarmament together by building partnerships at a national and global level. We can not have security amidst starvation and we cannot build peace without alleviating poverty and we cannot have either without a better environment. Only a peaceful society can work its way up to creating the institutions ripe for development and free itself from injustices and human rights abuses. The problems we face today – violent conflicts, destruction of nature, diseases, poverty and hunger – are human created problems which can be resolved through human effort, understanding and goodness.

- The global world institutions, democratically elected, endowed with limited but real powers could support solidarity and peace between the people of the world by establishing laws common to us all.

- We need collective will and determination to move ahead boldly to solve the pressing world problems of global governance and democracy facing us today.

- In a globalised world, where fundamentalism is rife, where there is a clash of culture and civilization, we need discussion and dialogue leading to inter-cultural and inter-religious harmony. We have to work to strike a balance between religious and secular values and forge a unity in this fragmented world. We need respect and tolerance between religious and different groups of people to treat each other with dignity.

- In the sphere of aid, we need to work for debt relief, doubling the aid for Africa and the implementation of Millennium Development Goals. Also improving emergency fund for responding to disasters.

# Fortune Forum Code

- In the area of peace and security, the General Assembly should adopt and reach an agreement to develop and implement a comprehensive global counter-terrorism strategy.

- Work for the success of the peacebuilding commission to help build countries emerging from violence and conflicts.

- Support the newly created human rights council for dealing more objectively and credibly with human rights violations. It should also adhere to human rights norms including dialogue and understanding among civilizations, cultures and religions.

- Work for the success of the ethics office, a democracy fund, and stronger protection for whistle blowers.

- A dialogue and understanding among civilizations, cultures, and religions can pave a way for a safer and brighter future.

- To work for promoting democracy and multilateralism which, paired with the rule of law, can deliver civil liberty, economic opportunity, and security which can change life in a positive way.

- For strengthening democratic institutions and development of pluralistic media, civil society should increase popular participation and ensure that people are able to exercise their democratic rights.

- To make reducing the global incidence of wars and military spending a new MDG. War retards development, but conversely, development retards war. Around 50% of the conflicts of the past 20 years have reoccurred within 5 years of the peace agreements. Getting rid of war is not a utopian dream. There already exists in the world large regions for example, European Union, within which war is inconceivable.

- To work towards using resources for peaceful and environmentally sustainable purposes. At present the global arms trade, and its accompanying glut of military spending, continues to represent the single most significant perversion of worldwide priorities known today. For the sixth year military spending rose to the trillion dollar mark while billions of people who never see more than $1 or $2 a day are held hostage to unconscionable poverty.

- To make the 21st century about governments giving power to the people. A united civil society (the new superpower) should use its strength for stopping politicians using their power unilaterally in violation of international law and multilateral treaties.

- For development to succeed, we must strive not to wage wars, but to win peace. Real peace must be built; it is not just the absence of war. We need to talk about the endgame, to develop understanding, to address the interdependent issues that is at the heart of so much instability, and to devise a multilateral approach to such thorny issues as the proliferation of WMD, together with a concept for human rights, prosperity and security.

We need governments and institutions which are transparent, democratic, accountable and can work together with NGOs and civil society. With all its weaknesses and need for reform, the UN is one of the best world institutions which has the clout, legitimacy and calibre to solve problems effectively on a world stage. All of these are problems that no one country, however powerful, can solve on its own and which are the shared responsibility of humankind.

Some of the examples of global development and governance can be listed as the newly formed International Criminal Court, Kyoto Protocol and MDGs where the governments of the world, NGOs and

# Fortune Forum Code

civil society have worked together certain common codes of conduct under which some of the challenges and threats including prosecution for crimes against humanity, protecting the environment and helping the poor to fight HIV/AIDs and poverty can be implemented globally.

We should celebrate our past achievements which are a result of successes of civil society brought by peace education. For example, Kyoto Protocol, NPT (Nuclear Non-Proliferation Treaty), UN Charter, Geneva Conventions, and the UDHR (Universal Declaration of Human Rights). Other achievements are abolition of slavery, freedom from colonialism, ending of apartheid, fall of the Berlin Wall and Magna Carta giving rights to ordinary people and initiating ideas of liberty, democracy and law.

## Tools to end global poverty

Putting an end to poverty goes far beyond building physical infrastructure and elevating per capita income in the developing world. While these advances are critical, it is equally necessary to help individuals gain control over key decisions in their lives. Humanitarian workers have learned that the surest way to put a dent in extreme poverty is to invest in women and girls. As their lives improve, they enhance the prospects of their families and entire communities.[38]

As a result of globalisation and, more recently, the unprecedented scale of humanitarian disasters and terrorist acts, people everywhere feel the world is shrinking. What happens in the remotest and poorest communities affects people everywhere. We understand this pragmatically and with a heightened awareness of our sameness.

---

[38] P. Hall, "We have the tools to end global poverty," The Christian Science Monitor, 22 March 2006.

# Vijay Mehta

It is clear that the goal of world development is to promote peace and security, protection of human rights and environment, rule of law, and uplifting the poorest regions of the world. If that can be put into action by leaders, civil society, and global institutions by linking the agenda of development, security and environment together, then we stand a fair chance of solving the huge problems of the 21st century.

But for all of us to reach that goal, powerful countries, institutions and individuals must continue to work to end violent conflict, social exclusion, hunger, illiteracy, and the scourge of disease. We resonate with the insight of Dr. Martin Luther King Jr: "In a real sense, all life is interrelated. The agony of the poor impoverishes the rich; the betterment of the poor enriches the rich."

## The world in 2006 and beyond

The year 2006 has seen the Iraq conflict sliding into a civil war, a war between Lebanon and Israel, thereby having vast repercussions for the Middle East. This will inevitably spill over to Europe and the wider world as tensions between the Muslim world and the rest become more intense. In Darfur, the best intention of the UN and the African Union failed to protect the population against gross abuses of international humanitarian law. The jury is out on security issues, as confrontation with North Korea and Iran is increasing by the day and may have disastrous consequences for international relations.

As far as the poorer countries are concerned, only a tiny ray of hope and accomplishment have been achieved as limited progress has been made in debt cancellation. The vast majority of children in sub-Sahara Africa still go to bed hungry every night while leaders of the rich countries were unable to put their differences aside and successfully complete the WTO Doha Round trade talks. Hence, no dates are agreed to phase out distorted subsidies on agricultural trade.

However, there is some good news as China and India become great economic powers with 8-10% annual growth in trade. China and India will become more self-confident and will project their own ideas on to concepts such as democracy, freedom and the rule of law. This has, however, created an insatiable demand for energy supplies (oil and gas) to continue this spectacular growth. This will certainly have a negative impact on the environment.

The world would be split along two axes; between democracies and autocracies; and between countries seeking a balance of power and those that want a world organised around international law and institutions. America will continue to be a powerful influence around the world. However, the falling dollar and an over militarised nation will diminish its status as the single superpower in the world.

According to The Economist, "The World in 2006", defence (military) spending will continue to rise. In America, this will rise by 5.00% to $419.3 billion while Russian is spending $24 billion. Against this huge military spending, the UN peacekeeping budget for the fiscal year 2005-06 is $3.2 billion. The strange paradox is that defence (military) spending is still counted as an industry like agriculture, banking or entertainment.

In recent times, climate change has worsened and for dealing with global warming, the signatories and non-signatories of the Kyoto Protocol have to come closer and take some concerted action to deal with the environment issue.

What we need in the world today is to accelerate growth and opportunities if we are to improve the lives of the world's poorest people. This should include a firm action plan to improve education, roads, infrastructure and also help with aid, debt cancellation and fairer trade. We have to empower poor people to take their destiny into their own hands.

On a positive note, the world leaders at the 2005 Summit agreed to have a Peacebuilding Commission and a Human Rights Council which are now functioning bodies. They also endorsed the concept of "responsibility to protect". It is the duty of the international community to make sure these institutions work for reducing conflicts, protecting human rights violations, and bringing a more peaceful and safer world.

### Comments on interdependent world

*Former US President Bill Clinton's comments on positive changes in an increasingly interdependent world[39]*

"The major mission of our time should be to move from an inheritably unstable and unequal interdependence, to a more integrated world locally, nationally and globally."

"What is keeping us from that sort of movement and what we need to do? I think that there are four challenges all of which have economic components and other components."

"There is a security challenge. It has been warped by overemphasis on what happened in Iraq. But there is a security challenge from terror, weapons of mass destruction, slaughter of innocents in place like Darfur and from the threat of global epidemics in an interdependent world."

"The second thing that I would like to talk briefly about is global

---

[39] B. Clinton, "The opportunity for private citizens to effect positive change in an increasingly interdependent world." London Business School, 28 March 2006

warming. I believe that it is the only existential threat that, those of you who are students here, your generation faces. It could literally undermine your ability to raise your children and grandchildren."

"The third thing you have to face is … equip yourself to do well and believe in the global economy over half the people are not benefiting from it. In the developing world, half the folks still live on $2 a day or less, a billion people on a dollar a day, a billion people go to bed hungry every night, a billion people have no access to clean water, 2.5 billion people have no access to sanitation, 1 in 4 deaths every year from AIDS, TB, Malaria, and infections related to unclean water mostly cholera and diarrhea."

"The final thing that I want to say is that private citizens have more power to do public good than ever before because of the rise of in the NGOs as a global movement in the developed and developing world alike."

"All we have to do it build a global community, an integrated global community, is to have people believe that every person is entitled to dignity and a chance, that competition is good but cooperation works better, that our differences are really important but our common humanity matters more."

# 8
# Ways for a better world

*Ideas for action, inspiration and timeless wisdom*

**May these ideas enter your being and resonate within you, so that you are awaken to action.**

**May the truth of these ideas awaken your logic, wisdom and compassion.**

**May it be the catalyst for action for achieving a world of peace and harmony.**

## Poverty and development

"Recall in the face of the poorest and most helpless person whom you may have seen and ask yourself if the step you contemplate is going to be of any use to him, will he gain anything by it? Will it restore him to control over his life and destiny? In other words, will it lead to swaraj[40], self-rule, for the hungry and also spiritually starved of our countrymen? Then you will find your doubts and yourself melting away."

"Be the change you want to see in the world."

"Almost everything you do will seem insignificant, but it is important that you do it."

---

[40] A sacred word, a Vedic word, meaning self-rule and self-restraint, and not freedom from all restraint which 'independence' often means.

# Fortune Forum Code

**Mahatma Gandhi** *(1869-1948) Indian leader of satyagraha, theory and practice of nonviolent resistance. He led the peaceful Indian resistance to British rule.*

"Like slavery and apartheid, poverty is not natural. It is man-made and it can be overcome and eradicated by the actions of human beings."

"Massive poverty and obscene inequality are such terrible scourges of our times that they have to rank alongside slavery and apartheid as social evils."
**Nelson Mandela,** *former South African President*

"Part of winning the war on terrorism is winning the war on poverty. We've had the wake-up call. If we stand by and watch [Africa] go up in flames, the price won't be paid solely in African lives."
**Bono,** *U2 lead singer*

"In our interconnected world a future built on the foundations of mass poverty in the midst of plenty is economically inefficient, politically unsustainable and morally indefensible."

"Today, for the first time in history, we have the means to end global poverty. All we need is will power and the resolve to do it."

"Completion of Millennium Development Goals[41] is essential for lifting millions out of poverty. Work together in unity, win the broadest sections of society to work for development."

---

[41] 1. Eradicate extreme poverty and hunger by half, 2. Achieve universal primary education, 3. Promote gender equality and empower women, 4. Reduce child mortality, 5. Improve maternal health, 6. Combat HIV/AIDS, malaria and other diseases, 7. Ensure environmental sustainability, 8. Develop a global partnership for development.

# Vijay Mehta

"Extreme inequality between countries and within countries is identified as one of the main barriers to human development and as a powerful brake on accelerated progress towards the MDGs."

"Recognise differences of people in society, respect of their ethnicity, religion, and language. Champion diversity and promote cultural freedoms, so that all people can choose to speak their language, practice their religion, and participate in shaping their culture."

"The range of human development in the world is vast and uneven, with astounding progress in some areas amidst stagnation and dismal decline in others. Balance and stability in the world will require the commitment of all nations, rich and poor, and a global development compact to extend the wealth of possibilities to all people for the completion of the MDGs."

"Politics is as important to successful development as economics. Sustained poverty reduction requires equitable growth-but it also requires that poor people have political power for building strong and deep forms of democratic governance at all levels of society."

"Make human rights compulsory principles of accountability and social justice to the process of human development."

"Being global markets, global technology, global ideas and global solidarity which can enrich the lives of people everywhere and the benefits are shared equitably".

"Harness the power and potential of technology and information which present great opportunities."

"Eradicating poverty everywhere is more than a moral imperative - it is a practical possibility. The world has the resources and the know-how to create a poverty-free world in less than a generation."

"The quality of economic growth, if not properly managed, can be jobless, voiceless, ruthless, rootless and futureless, and thus detrimental to human development."
**Vijay Mehta**

### Environment

"There is a sufficiency in the world for man's need but not for man's greed."
**Mahatma Gandhi**

"Our reservoir of life is shrinking. Before it is too late I think we need to put our environmental house in order."
**Mikhail Gorbachev,** *former Soviet leader*

"The key is actually discarding the idea that has dominated economic policy-making, which is: in order for a country to get rich, stay rich and get richer, you have to put more greenhouse gases in the atmosphere. That isn't true and it hasn't been true for years."
**Bill Clinton,** *former US President*

"The supreme reality of our time is...the vulnerability of our planet"
**John F. Kennedy,** *former US President*

"The environment is very important in the aspects of peace because when we destroy our resources, they become scarce and we fight over that."
**Wangari Maathai,** *environmentalist and awarded the Nobel Prize*

"Only when the last tree has died and the last river been poisoned and

the last fish been caught will we realise we cannot eat money."
**Cree Indian Proverb**

"Because we don't think about future generations, they will never forget us."
**Henrik Tikkanen,** *Finnish author and artist*

"We do not inherit the earth from our ancestors, we borrow it from our children."
**Native American Proverb**

"Destroying rainforest for economic gain is like burning a Renaissance painting to cook a meal."
**Edward Wilson,** *explorer and physician*

"Look deep into nature, and then you will understand everything better."
**Albert Einstein,** *(1879-1955) physicist and awarded the Nobel Prize, 1922*

"If you live according to nature, you never will be poor; if according to the world's caprice, you will never be rich."
**Publilius Syrus (42 BC),** *Latin writer*

"Nature uses as little as possible of anything."
**Johannes Kepler**, *German mathematician and astronomer*

"Nature does nothing uselessly."
**Aristotle** *Greek philosopher*

"Men argue; nature acts."
**Voltaire** *French writer*

# Fortune Forum Code

"After a visit to the beach, it's hard to believe that we live in a material world."
**Pam Shaw**, *author*


"This curious world which we inhabit is more wonderful than it is convenient, more beautiful than it is useful; it is more to be admired and enjoyed than used."
**Henry David Thoreau**, American writer (1817-1862)


"If we once, and for so long, lived in balance with nature and each other, we should be able to do so again."
**John Zerzan***, American philosopher*


"In the United Kingdom no one lives more than 75 miles from the sea. For us, as an island nation, the sea has an all-embracing presence. Spiritually and physically we are intimately connected with our shores. The sea has immense power, which we ignore at our peril."
**National Trust** *'Shifting Shores - Living with a changing coastline' (2005)*


"The question facing the world's governments, businesses and green groups is thus not simply how best to tackle the world's growing environmental crisis, but how to do so in a manner that does not at the same time hamstring national economies, especially those of the world's poorest nations."


"Environmental destruction, population growth and poverty are intricately connected. Aid from industrialised nations and internal education and reform are both needed. A new world view in which all things are seen as connected and all human beings are equal is the ultimate solution."

# Vijay Mehta

"To work for environmental protection to make a contribution to the world by teaching the importance of caring, sharing and living in harmony, and bring forth the inherent dignity of the individual."

"Energy security will not become a reality without diversification, which most importantly means the expansion of types of energy in use into low-carbon alternative power, renewables, and innovations."
**Vijay Mehta**

## Disease

"The global HIV/AIDS epidemic is an unprecedented crisis that requires an unprecedented response. In particular it requires solidarity -- between the healthy and the sick, between rich and poor, and above all, between richer and poorer nations. We have 30 million orphans already. How many more do we have to get, to wake up?"
**Kofi Annan,** *(1938- ) Secretary-General of the United Nations.*

"It's time to make the connection between debt relief and epidemic relief. If the international community relieves some of their external debt, these countries can reinvest the savings in poverty alleviation and AIDS prevention and care. If not, poverty will just continue to fan the flames of the epidemic."
**Peter Piot,** *Executive Director of UNAIDS*

"It's really a tragedy that the world has done so little to stop this disease that kills 2,000 African children every day,"
**Bill Gates** *Founder, Microsoft*

"AIDS and malaria and TB are national security issues. A worldwide program to get a start on dealing with these issues would cost about $25 billion... It's, what, a few months in Iraq."
**Jared Diamond** *Writer*

# Fortune Forum Code

"This is a crucial moment in the history of HIV/AIDS, and an unprecedented opportunity to alter its course. The international community has the chance to change the history of health for generations to come and to open the door to better health for all."

"What is needed now is political will to implement national plans, together with international cooperation to align resources, harness knowledge and build robust health systems for treating and preventing disease and promoting population health."
**Vijay Mehta**


## Peace and Education

"All humanity is one undivided and indivisible family, and each one of us is responsible for the misdeeds of all others."

"If we are to teach real peace in the world we shall have to begin with children."

"There is no way to peace. Peace is the way."
**Mahatma Gandhi**

"Since wars begin in the minds of men, it is in the minds of men that the defences of peace must be constructed."
**UNESCO,** *Declaration of a culture of peace*

"I have been asked a question many a time, 'who is your hero?' I say, my hero does not depend on the position a person occupies. My heroes are those simple men and women who have committed themselves to fighting poverty wherever that is to be found in the world."
**Nelson Mandela**

# Vijay Mehta

"You cannot simultaneously prevent and prepare for war."

"War cannot be humanised. It can only be abolished."
**Albert Einstein**

"Sometimes there's truth in old cliches. There can be no real peace without justice. And without resistance there will be no justice."
**Arundhati Roy,** *Indian writer*

"All war represents a failure of diplomacy."
**Tony Benn,** *retired British MP*

"If the world could end apartheid the world can end war."
**Archbishop (Ret.) Desmond Tutu** *(1931- ) Johannesburg, South Africa, founder of the Truth and Reconciliation Commission, awarded the Nobel Peace Prize 1984.*

"Wars make poor tools for carving out peaceful tomorrows."

"It is not the violence of a few that scares me, it is the silence of the many"
**Martin Luther King, Jr.** *(1929-1968) U.S. Christian Minister and leader of the U.S. civil rights movement, awarded the Nobel Peace Prize, 1964.*

"We cannot have it both ways. We can't be both the world's leading champion of peace and the world's leading supplier of arms."
**Jimmy Carter,** *former US President.*

"War must cease to be an admissible human institution. The abolition of all war must be our ultimate goal."

"For the concept of a war-free world to become universally accepted

and consciously adopted by making war illegal, a process of education will be required at all levels; education for peace, education for world citizenship. war is not an inherent element in human society."
**Sir Joseph Rotblat** *(1908-2005), Nobel Peace Prize, 1995.*

"In this new century, we must start from the understanding that peace belongs not only to states or peoples, but to each and every member of those communities. Peace must be made real and tangible in the daily existence of every individual in need. Peace must be sought, above all, because it is the condition for every member of the human family to live a life of dignity and security."

"There is no trust more sacred than the one the world holds with children. There is no duty more important than ensuring that their rights are respected, that their welfare is protected, that their lives are free from fear and want and that they grow up in peace."
**Kofi Annan**

"Peace begins when the hungry are fed."
**Anonymous**

"It isn't enough to talk about peace. One must believe in it. And it isn't enough to believe in it. One must work at it."
**Eleanor Roosevelt** *(1884-1962), American human rights activist, stateswoman; First Lady of the United States (1933-1945).*

"The pacifist's task today is to find a method of helping and healing which provides a revolutionary constructive substitute for war."
**Vera Brittain,** *(1893-1970) Pacifist, best known for her book Testament of Youth.*

"Local, regional and world leaders must accept the fact that we cannot let the free market rule the international arms trade. We must not enrich ourselves through the commerce of death. Rather, we must realise that the arms trade is most often a friend of dictators and an enemy of the people. The time has come to choose human lives over arms."

"Peace is not the product of a victory or a command. it has no finishing line, no final deadline, no fixed definition of achievement. Peace is a never-ending process, the work of many decisions. "
**Dr Oscar Arias**, *Nobel Peace Prize Laureate, 1987.*

"A culture of peace will be achieved when citizens of the world understand global problems; have the skills to resolve conflict constructively; know and live by international standards of human rights, gender and racial equality; appreciate cultural diversity; and respect the integrity of the Earth. Such learning can not be achieved without intentional, sustained and systematic education for peace."
**Global Campaign for Peace Education.**

"Militarism must be recognised as idolatry. The way in which it is looked at shows that it is more than a system and even an ideology."
**World Council of Churches** *(WCC), Report of the Consultation on Militarism and Disarmament (1989)*

"To tackle the underlying roots of violence and conflict, we need a massive international effort to reduce poverty and injustice, and to promote development, democracy and human rights."
**Clare Short,** *Former UK International Development secretary*

"Nothing can bring you peace but yourself."
**Ralph Waldo Emerson** *Writer*

"If we have no peace, it is because we have forgotten that we belong to each other."
**Mother Teresa** *Nun & Nobel Prize Winner*

# Fortune Forum Code

"All education is for peace."

"Establishing lasting peace is the work of education; all politics can do is keep us out of war."
**Maria Montessori,** *Italian philosopher and physician*

"To suggest that war can prevent war is a base play on words and a despicable form of warmongering. The world has had ample evidence that war begets only conditions that beget further war.
**Ralph Bunche,** *American diplomat*

"Imagine all the people living life in peace. You may say I'm a dreamer, but I'm not the only one. I hope someday you'll join us, and the world will be as one."
**John Lennon** *Former Beatles band member*

"More than an end to war, we want an end to the beginning of all wars – yes, an end to this brutal, inhuman and thoroughly impractical method of settling the differences between governments."
**Franklin D. Roosevelt** *Former US President*

"These are all our children. We will all profit by, or pay for, whatever they become."
**James Baldwin,** *author*

"Our children and grandchildren – and unborn generations to come – are depending on us…to make the wise decisions that will determine their future. The choice is in our hands.
**James P. Grant,** *former executive director of UNICEF*

"No one has yet realized the wealth of sympathy, the kindness and generosity hidden in the soul of a child."
**Emma Goldman,** *Lithuanian anarchist*

# Vijay Mehta

"To have peace we must end economic and military competition and acknowledge our planetary interconnections and must consider the needs of all humankind."

"The Culture of Peace consists of values, attitudes and behaviours that reject violence. In a peaceful world, we solve problems through dialogue and negotiation."

"The key to peace is reaching out and educating the youth, as they are the next generation who can ensure a more peaceful future for the world."

"What use is war? Let us all work together for peace and non-violence."

"To me culture of peace is a set of values, attitudes and ways of life based on principles of freedom, equality, justice, tolerance, solidarity, and human dignity. By forging together respect for diversity, dialogue and understanding we can bring about the transformation from a culture of war to a culture of peace."

"Peace education should be linked to the wider expression of ideas."

"Peace hero's, rather then military hero's, should be made more visible in our cities, monuments and museums."

"Peace begins when the hungry are fed, poor are clothed, children are fearless, human rights are protected, non-violence becomes a way of life and human dignity and justice prevails"

"The ultimate purpose of education is to serve and benefit humanity by developing qualities of love, compassion, generosity and tolerance."

# Fortune Forum Code

"Teaching peace takes a lot of time and hard work. But if you continue and keep the goal in mind then Global peace, harmony and happiness can not be far away."

"The best way to educate and get the message to the illiterate is through music and the visual arts. Art should be used to tear down road blocks and pave the way for progress."

"Global public opinion is considered a superpower in its own right. We have a responsibility to use it in a positive way for a just, peaceful and sustainable future."

"Peace education in schools is essential and through a national database, can be used as a way of networking and informing the general public. At a global level, the role of UNESCO is important to spread its message of a *culture of peace* to overcome violence and conflicts."

"Moving from a culture of war a culture of peace means vast internal transformations in individuals as well as nations. We must move from an era of cultural imperialism, in which powerful nations impose their will on weaker countries, to an era of cultural exchange and respect."
**Vijay Mehta**


## Disarmament

"Every gun that is made, every warship launched, every rocket fired, represents, in the final analysis, a theft from those who hunger and are not fed, who are cold and are not clothed. This world in arms is not spending money alone. It is spending the sweat of its laborers, the genius of its scientists, the hopes of its children."
**Dwight Eisenhower**, *General Commander Allied Forces, World*

# Vijay Mehta

*War 2 and US President, 1952-60.*

"I know not with what weapons World War III will be fought, but World War IV will be fought with sticks and stones."
**Albert Einstein**

"The life of active nonviolence is the fruit of an inner peace and spiritual unity…"
**Mairead Maguire,** *peace activist and co-received Nobel Peace prize with Betty Williams*

"Religion is essentially the art and the theory of the remaking of man. Man is not a finished creation."
**Edmund Burke,** *English philosopher*

"Call for the dismantling of the institution of war just as the world has abolished the institutions of slavery, colonialism and apartheid."

"Ultimately, we must end our reliance on weapons. Ending our trust in arms is the only way to bring trust among peoples. The solidarity and action of common people can bring about total disarmament."

"Working for the abolition of nuclear weapons has a strong moral basis. It has the truth and humanity on its side. There is no such thing as 'overriding' morality."

"Divert the $1000 billion military spending and instead feed, house and educate all the peoples of this world."

"Global norms for disarmament are vital to the sustainable development, quality of life, and ultimately the survival of this planet."

# Fortune Forum Code

"Sowing the seed of peace for the next generation of leaders requires educating today's younger generation the value of coexistence, respect and human dignity for each other."

"Demilitarise the global economy by reducing military budgets and shifting resources toward human security programs."

"Things we need to do is dialogue, discussion, diplomacy, and disarmament for peace and harmony."
**Vijay Mehta**


## Timeless wisdoms

"If you think you are too small to change the world, try sleeping with a mosquito."

"Love, compassion and tolerance are necessities of life. Without them humanity cannot survive."
**Dalai Lama**, *Spiritual Leader of Tibet*

"As human beings, our greatness lies not so much in being able to remake the world, as in being able to remake ourselves."
**Mahatma Gandhi**

"It is not power that corrupts, but fear. Fear of losing power corrupts those who wield it and fear of the scourge of power corrupts those who are subject to it."
**Aung San Suu Kyi** *(1945- ) Nobel Peace Prize, 1991.*

"Never doubt that a small group of thoughtful, committed citizens can change the world; indeed, it is the only thing that ever has."
**Margaret Mead,** *American cultural anthropologist*

# Vijay Mehta

"If you are neutral in situations of injustice, you have chosen the side of the oppressor."

"The good we secure for ourselves is precarious and uncertain until it is secured for all of us and incorporated into our common life."
**Jane Addams** *(1860-1935) Nobel Peace Prize, 1931*

"In separateness lies the world's great misery; in compassion lies the world's true strength."
**The Buddha**. *Founder of the Buddhist philosophy, born around 565 B.C. in Nepal. Buddha means "enlightened one".*

"I believe that the widespread use of cross-cultural dialogue will foster the global community we so earnestly seek."
**Michael Nobel,** *consultant to UNESCO and great grandson to Alfred Nobel*

"Teaching our children to treat others as they wish to be treated is one of the most fundamental values we adults can pass on. We would have a different country and world if this lesson was learned and followed."
**Marian Wright Edelman,** *president and founder of Children's Defence Fund*

"Heroism has nothing to do with skin color or social status. It is a state of mind and a willingness to act for what is right and just."
**Maya Angelou**, *American poet*

"I hear people talking about the community, and I stop and think and I feel that we each use a different language. Community means balance."
**Rigoberta Menchu Tum**, *indigenous Guatemalan and recipient of the Nobel Peace prize*

# Fortune Forum Code

"At a time when people of very different traditions, faiths and ideals have come into sudden and close contact with one another, the survival of humankind requires that people be willing to live with one another and to accept that there is more than one path to truth and salvation."
**Arnold Toynbee**, *historian*

"A single, all-embracing global civilization has arisen."
**Vaclav Havel,** *former President, Czech Republic*

"If you are neutral in situations of injustice, you have chosen the side of the oppressor. If an elephant has its foot on the tail of a mouse and you say that you are neutral, the mouse will not appreciate your neutrality."
**Archbishop (Ret.) Desmond Tutu**

"The love of one's country is a splendid thing. But why should love stop at the border?"
**Pablo Casals**, *Spanish cellist*

"Our human situation no longer permits us to make armed dichotomies between those who are good and those who are evil, those who are right and those who are wrong. The first blow dealt to the enemy's children will sign the death warrant of our own."
**Margaret Mead**

"Throughout history, religious differences have divided men and women from their neighbours and have served as justification for some of humankind's bloodiest conflicts. In the modern world, it has become clear that people of all religions must bridge these differences and work together, to ensure our survival and realize the vision of peace that all faiths share."
**H.R.H. Prince El-Hassan bin Talal, of Jordan**

# Vijay Mehta

"The foremost treasure of sentient beings is none other than life itself…When you light the path before another person you brighten your own."
**Buddhist – Nichiren**

"Do not do to others what you do not want them to do to you."
**Confucius – Analects**

"You shall love your neighbour as yourself."
**Jewish – Leviticus**

"A person should treat all creatures as he himself would be treated."
**Jainism – Sutraktanga**

"Not one of you is a believer until he loves for his brother what he loves for himself."
**Islam - Fourth Hadith of an-Nawawi**

"Therefore all things whatsoever ye would that men should do to you, do ye even so to them."
**Christian – Matthew**

"This is the sum of duty: do nothing to others which would cause you pain if done to you."
**Hindu – Mahabharata**

"Youth is the first victim of war, the first fruit of peace. It takes twenty years or more of peace to make a man; it takes only twenty seconds of war to destroy him."
**King Baudouin I, King of Belgium**


People are often unreasonable, illogical, and self-centered;
Forgive them anyway.

# Fortune Forum Code

If you are kind, People may Accuse you of Selfish, Ulterior motives;
Be kind anyway.
If you are successful, you will win some false friends and some true
enemies;
Succeed anyway.
If you are honest and frank, people may cheat you;
Be Honest and Frank anyway.
What you spend years building, someone could destroy overnight;
Build anyway.
If you find serenity and happiness, they may be jealous;
Be happy anyway.
The good you do today, people will often forget tomorrow;
Do good anyway.
Give the world the best you have,
and it may never be enough;
Give the world the best you've got anyway.
You see, in the final analysis,
it is between you and God;
It was never between you and them anyway.
**Mother Teresa**

"What will the role of nations be in the new millennium? Work for
equality, mutual respect and peaceful coexistence."

"There are dozens of major religions in the world and thousands of
belief systems by which people guide their lives, design ethical codes
and find happiness. Learn to use one another's religious beliefs as a
way to connect, no as reasons for conflict."

"All spiritual teachings and religions of the world call for universal
and eternal truths of love, peace, kindness and harmony. They call to
promote self control, sacrifice, harmony, non-violence and
understanding. Follow their teachings, all conflicts can be avoided
and we can create a heaven on earth."

# Vijay Mehta

"Humanity needs hero's, exemplary human beings, who set forth on a lonely and frightening quest. But eventually they bring something of immense value to our society. We need such hero's to change the course of history, by bringing holistic, multilateral and universal approach to the ills of our society."

"No peace without justice. No justice without forgiveness and no forgiveness without compassion."

"Among many prerequisite, in a situation of conflict resolution, are meaningful dialogue, active listening, honest conversation, accepting the other's view without agreeing or disagreeing, and acknowledging the other's pain."

"In today's world there is a dire need of ethical and multi-faith dialogue. There are common values that human beings share, irrespective of religion, nationality or ethnicity."

"Everyone will be judged by their intentions and actions. A small body of determined spirits fired by an unquenchable faith in their mission can alter the course of history."

"End violence against women in times of armed conflict and stop the use of child soldiers."

"Protect human rights defenders, humanitarian workers and whistleblowers."

"Promote increased public knowledge, teaching and understanding and enforcement mechanism for enforcement of international law and human rights."

# Fortune Forum Code

"Build upon the successes and failures of truth commissions and political amnesties."

"Establish a universal and effective system of Habeas Corpus."

"Subject warmaking to democratic controls and strengthen the United Nations' capacity to maintain peace."

"Prioritise early warning and early response in situation of conflict. Promote the training of civilian peace professionals."

"Utilise the media as a proactive tool for peacebuilding and promote for the implementation of a global action plan to prevent war."

"Be kind, respect the Earth, walk in a forest, plant a tree and speak for a healthy planet."

"Support the United Nations, the International Criminal Court and read and act out the Universal Declaration of Human Rights."

"Be constructive, let someone else go first, plant seeds of peace, change a potential enemy into a friend, be positive."

"Send sunflowers to world leaders, and call for a world free of armaments and conflicts."

"Oppose technologies that harm the environment."

"Value diversity, walk softly on the Earth, appreciate the power of the sun, and speak out for global disarmament."

"Perhaps only deep conviction with a morally-based vision can open the gates to a rational and truly democratic new world order."

"The seed, hidden in the heart of an apple, is an orchard invisible."

# Vijay Mehta

"Halt the decline of morality, the absence of truth and virtue - bring back the lost path of righteousness."

"Traveller, there is no Path. Paths are made by Walking."

"Every one is a drop that makes the ocean"
**Vijay Mehta**

# Appendices

.

Vijay Mehta

Fortune Forum Code

# UN Charter, preamble

***WE THE PEOPLES OF THE UNITED NATIONS
DETERMINED***

- to save succeeding generations from the scourge of war, which twice in our lifetime has brought untold sorrow to mankind, and

- to reaffirm faith in fundamental human rights, in the dignity and worth of the human person, in the equal rights of men and women and of nations large and small, and

- to establish conditions under which justice and respect for the obligations arising from treaties and other sources of international law can be maintained, and

- to promote social progress and better standards of life in larger freedom,

***AND FOR THESE ENDS***

- to practice tolerance and live together in peace with one another as good neighbours, and

- to unite our strength to maintain international peace and security, and

- to ensure, by the acceptance of principles and the institution of methods, that armed force shall not be used, save in the common interest, and

- to employ international machinery for the promotion of the economic and social advancement of all peoples,

*HAVE RESOLVED TO COMBINE OUR EFFORTS TO ACCOMPLISH THESE AIMS*

Accordingly, our respective Governments, through representatives assembled in the city of San Francisco, who have exhibited their full powers found to be in good and due form, have agreed to the present Charter of the United Nations and do hereby establish an international organization to be known as the United Nations.

# Universal Declaration of Human Rights, preamble

*Adopted and proclaimed by General Assembly resolution 217 A (III) of 10 December 1948*

**On December 10, 1948 the General Assembly of the United Nations adopted and proclaimed the Universal Declaration of Human Rights the full text of which appears in the following pages. Following this historic act the Assembly called upon all Member countries to publicize the text of the Declaration and 'to cause it to be disseminated, displayed, read and expounded principally in schools and other educational institutions, without distinction based on the political status of countries or territories.'**

## *PREAMBLE*

Whereas recognition of the inherent dignity and of the equal and inalienable rights of all members of the human family is the foundation of freedom, justice and peace in the world,

Whereas disregard and contempt for human rights have resulted in barbarous acts which have outraged the conscience of mankind, and the advent of a world in which human beings shall enjoy freedom of speech and belief and freedom from fear and want has been proclaimed as the highest aspiration of the common people,

Whereas it is essential, if man is not to be compelled to have recourse, as a last resort, to rebellion against tyranny and oppression, that human rights should be protected by the rule of law,

Whereas it is essential to promote the development of friendly relations between nations,

Whereas the peoples of the United Nations have in the Charter reaffirmed their faith in fundamental human rights, in the dignity and worth of the human person and in the equal rights of men and women and have determined to promote social progress and better standards of life in larger freedom,

Whereas Member States have pledged themselves to achieve, in co-operation with the United Nations, the promotion of universal respect for and observance of human rights and fundamental freedoms,

Whereas a common understanding of these rights and freedoms is of the greatest importance for the full realization of this pledge,

**Now, Therefore THE GENERAL ASSEMBLY proclaims THIS UNIVERSAL DECLARATION OF HUMAN RIGHTS** as a common standard of achievement for all peoples and all nations, to the end that every individual and every organ of society, keeping this Declaration constantly in mind, shall strive by teaching and education to promote respect for these rights and freedoms and by progressive measures, national and international, to secure their universal and effective recognition and observance, both among the peoples of Member States themselves and among the peoples of territories under their jurisdiction.

**SPECIFIC UDHR ARTICLES on POVERTY and HUMAN RIGHTS:**

*Article 22.*

Everyone, as a member of society, has the right to social security and is entitled to realization, through national effort and international co-operation and in accordance with the organization and resources of each State, of the economic, social and cultural rights indispensable for his dignity and the free development of his personality.

## *Article 23.*

(1) Everyone has the right to work, to free choice of employment, to just and favourable conditions of work and to protection against unemployment.

(2) Everyone, without any discrimination, has the right to equal pay for equal work.

(3) Everyone who works has the right to just and favourable remuneration ensuring for himself and his family an existence worthy of human dignity, and supplemented, if necessary, by other means of social protection.

(4) Everyone has the right to form and to join trade unions for the protection of his interests.

## *Article 24.*

Everyone has the right to rest and leisure, including reasonable limitation of working hours and periodic holidays with pay.

## *Article 25.*

(1) Everyone has the right to a standard of living adequate for the health and well-being of himself and of his family, including food, clothing, housing and medical care and necessary social services, and the right to security in the event of unemployment, sickness, disability, widowhood, old age or other lack of livelihood in circumstances beyond his control.

(2) Motherhood and childhood are entitled to special care and assistance. All children, whether born in or out of wedlock, shall enjoy the same social protection.

*Article 26.*

(1) Everyone has the right to education. Education shall be free, at least in the elementary and fundamental stages. Elementary education shall be compulsory. Technical and professional education shall be made generally available and higher education shall be equally accessible to all on the basis of merit.

(2) Education shall be directed to the full development of the human personality and to the strengthening of respect for human rights and fundamental freedoms. It shall promote understanding, tolerance and friendship among all nations, racial or religious groups, and shall further the activities of the United Nations for the maintenance of peace.

(3) Parents have a prior right to choose the kind of education that shall be given to their children.

*Article 27.*

(1) Everyone has the right freely to participate in the cultural life of the community, to enjoy the arts and to share in scientific advancement and its benefits.

(2) Everyone has the right to the protection of the moral and material interests resulting from any scientific, literary or artistic production of which he is the author.

# UN Millennium Development Goals

---

### Goal 1: Eradicate extreme poverty and hunger

**Target 1**: Halve, between 1990 and 2015, the proportion of people whose income is less than one dollar a day

**1.** Proportion of population below $1 per day
**2.** Poverty gap ratio [incidence x depth of poverty]
**3.** Share of poorest quintile in national consumption

**Target 2**: Halve, between 1990 and 2015, the proportion of people who suffer from hunger
**4.** Prevalence of underweight children (under-five years of age)
**5.** Proportion of population below minimum level of dietary energy consumption

### Goal 2: Achieve universal primary education

**Target 3**: Ensure that, by 2015, children everywhere, boys and girls alike, will be able to complete a full course of primary schooling
**6.** Net enrolment ratio in primary education
**7.** Proportion of pupils starting grade 1 who reach grade 5
**8.** Literacy rate of 15-24 year olds

### Goal 3: Promote gender equality and empower women

**Target 4**: Eliminate gender disparity in primary and secondary education preferably by 2005 and to all levels of education no later than 2015
**9.** Ratio of girls to boys in primary, secondary and tertiary education
**10.** Ratio of literate females to males of 15-24 year olds

# Vijay Mehta

**11.** Share of women in wage employment in the nonagricultural sector

**12.** Proportion of seats held by women in national parliament

## Goal 4: Reduce child mortality

**Target 5**: Reduce by two-thirds, between 1990 and 2015, the under-five mortality rate

**13.** Under-five mortality rate

**14.** Infant mortality rate

**15.** Proportion of 1 year old children immunised against measles

## Goal 5: Improve maternal health

**Target 6**: Reduce by three-quarters, between 1990 and 2015, the maternal mortality ratio

**16.** Maternal mortality ratio

**17.** Proportion of births attended by skilled health personnel

## Goal 6: Combat HIV/AIDS, malaria and other diseases

**Target 7**: Have halted by 2015, and begun to reverse, the spread of HIV/AIDS

**18.** HIV prevalence among 15-24 year old pregnant women

**19.** Contraceptive prevalence rate

**20.** Number of children orphaned by HIV/AIDS

**Target 8**: Have halted by 2015, and begun to reverse, the incidence of malaria and other major diseases

**21.** Prevalence and death rates associated with malaria

**22.** Proportion of population in malaria risk areas using effective malaria prevention and treatment measures

**23.** Prevalence and death rates associated with tuberculosis

**24.** Proportion of TB cases detected and cured under DOTS

# Fortune Forum Code
(Directly Observed Treatment Short Course)

## Goal 7: Ensure environmental sustainability

**Target 9**: Integrate the principles of sustainable development into country policies and programmes and reverse the loss of environmental resources
**25.** Proportion of land area covered by forest
**26.** Land area protected to maintain biological diversity
**27.** GDP per unit of energy use (as proxy for energy efficiency)
**28.** Carbon dioxide emissions (per capita)
[Plus two figures of global atmospheric pollution: ozone depletion and the accumulation of global warming gases]

**Target 10**: Halve, by 2015, the proportion of people without sustainable access to safe drinking water
**29.** Proportion of population with sustainable access to an improved water source

**Target 11**: By 2020, to have achieved a significant improvement in the lives of at least 100 million slum dwellers
**30.** Proportion of people with access to improved sanitation
**31.** Proportion of people with access to secure tenure
[Urban/rural disaggregation of several of the above indicators may be relevant for monitoring improvement in the lives of slum dwellers]

## Goal 8: Develop a Global Partnership for Development

**Target 12**: Develop further an open, rule-based, predictable, non-discriminatory trading and financial system. Includes a commitment to good governance, development, and poverty reduction – both nationally and internationally

**Target 13**: Address the Special Needs of the Least Developed Countries
Includes: tariff and quota free access for LDC exports; enhanced programme of debt relief for HIPC and cancellation of official bilateral debt; and more generous ODA for countries committed to poverty reduction

**Target 14:** Address the Special Needs of landlocked countries and small island developing states (through Barbados Programme and 22nd General Assembly provisions)

**Target 15:** Deal comprehensively with the debt problems of developing countries through national and international measures in order to make debt sustainable in the long term
*Some of the indicators listed below will be monitored separately for the Least Developed Countries (LDCs), Africa, landlocked countries and small island developing states. Official Development Assistance*
**32.** Net ODA as percentage of DAC donors' GNI [targets of
0.7% in total and 0.15% for LDCs]
**33.** Proportion of ODA to basic social services (basic education, primary health care, nutrition, safe water and sanitation)
**34.** Proportion of ODA that is untied
**35.** Proportion of ODA for environment in small island developing states
**36.** Proportion of ODA for transport sector in land-locked countries
*Market Access*
**37.** Proportion of exports (by value and excluding arms) admitted free of duties and quotas
**38.** Average tariffs and quotas on agricultural products and textiles and clothing
**39.** Domestic and export agricultural subsidies in OECD countries
**40.** Proportion of ODA provided to help build trade capacity
*Debt Sustainability*
**41.** Proportion of official bilateral HIPC debt cancelled

# Fortune Forum Code

**42.** Debt service as a percentage of exports of goods and services
**43.** Proportion of ODA provided as debt relief
**44.** Number of countries reaching HIPC decision and completion points

**Target 16:** In co-operation with developing countries, develop and implement strategies for decent and productive work for youth
**45.** Unemployment rate of 15-24 year olds

**Target 17:** In co-operation with pharmaceutical companies, provide access to affordable, essential drugs in developing countries
**46.** Proportion of population with access to affordable essential drugs on a sustainable basis

**Target 18:** In co-operation with the private sector, make available the benefits of new technologies, especially information and communications
**47.** Telephone lines per 1000 people
**48.** Personal computers per 1000 people

Vijay Mehta

# Investing in Development

---

## Introduction

We have the opportunity in the coming decade to cut world poverty by half. Billions more people could enjoy the fruits of the global economy. Tens of millions of lives can be saved. The practical solutions exist. The political framework is established. And for the first time, the cost is utterly affordable. Whatever one's motivation for attacking the crisis of extreme poverty—human rights, religious values, security, fiscal prudence, ideology—the solutions are the same. All that is needed is action.

This report recommends the way forward. It outlines a way to attain this bold ambition. It describes how to achieve the Millennium Development Goals.

The Millennium Development Goals (MDGs) are the world's time-bound and quantified targets for addressing extreme poverty in its many dimensions— income poverty, hunger, disease, lack of adequate shelter, and exclusion— while promoting gender equality, education, and environmental sustainability. They are also basic human rights—the rights of each person on the planet to health, education, shelter, and security as pledged in the Universal Declaration of Human Rights and the UN Millennium Declaration.

How will the world look in 2015 if the Goals are achieved? More than 500 million people will be lifted out of extreme poverty. More than 300 million will no longer suffer from hunger. There will also be dramatic progress in child health. Rather than die before reaching their fifth birthdays, 30 million children will be saved. So will the

156

lives of more than 2 million mothers.

There's more. Achieving the Goals will mean 350 million fewer people are without safe drinking water and 650 million fewer people live without the benefits of basic sanitation, allowing them to lead healthier and more dignified lives. Hundreds of millions more women and girls will go to school, access economic and political opportunity, and have greater security and safety. Behind these large numbers are the lives and hopes of people seeking new opportunities to end the burden of grinding poverty and contribute to economic growth and renewal.

Many countries are on track to achieve at least some of the Goals by the appointed year, 2015. Yet broad regions are far off track (table 1). Sub-Saharan Africa, most dramatically, has been in a downward spiral of AIDS, resurgent malaria, falling food output per person, deteriorating shelter conditions, and environmental degradation, so that most countries in Africa are far off track to achieve most or all of the Goals. Climate change could worsen the situation by increasing food insecurity, spreading vector-borne diseases, and increasing the likelihood of natural disasters, while a prolonged decline in rainfall in parts of Africa has already wreaked havoc. Meanwhile, for some Goals, such as reducing maternal mortality and reversing the loss of environmental resources, most of the world is off track. The early target for gender parity in primary and secondary education—with a deadline of 2005—will be missed in many countries.

The Millennium Development Goals are too important to fail. It is time to put them on the fast-track they require and deserve. The year 2005 should inaugurate a decade of bold action. Based on work conducted by more than 250 of the world's leading development practitioners over the past two years in the context of the UN Millennium Project, this report presents a practical plan for achieving the Goals. Throughout, we stress that the specific technologies for achieving the Goals are known. What is needed is to apply them at scale. To that end, we present 10 key recommendations at the front of the report. More elaborate analysis and recommendations are set out in the 13 thematically oriented task force reports that underpin this plan.

This overview has four parts.[42] The first describes why the Millennium Development Goals are important and the varied progress so far in achieving them. It then offers a diagnosis of why progress has been so mixed across regions and across Goals. The second presents the recommendations to be implemented at the country level, focusing on the processes, investments, policies, and scale-up strategies required to achieve the Goals. The third provides recommendations to guide the international system's support for country-level processes. The fourth estimates the costs and benefits of achieving the Goals, outlining the millions of lives that could be saved—and the billions of lives improved—through a very affordable but substantial increase in worldwide investments.

## Why the Goals are important and why we're falling short

The Millennium Development Goals are the most broadly supported, comprehensive, and specific poverty reduction targets the world has ever established, so their importance is manifold. For the international political system, they are the fulcrum on which development policy is based. For the billion-plus people living in extreme poverty, they represent the means to a productive life. For everyone on Earth, they are a linchpin to the quest for a more secure and peaceful world.

---

[42] To view all four parts of the overview of 'Investing in Development', see the link
http://www.unmillenniumproject.org/reports

# Fortune Forum Code

## The fulcrum of international development policy

At the Millennium Summit in September 2000, the largest gathering of world leaders in history adopted the UN Millennium Declaration, committing their nations to a global partnership to reduce poverty, improve health, and promote peace, human rights, gender equality, and environmental sustainability. Soon after, world leaders met again at the March 2002 International Conference on Financing for Development in Monterrey, Mexico, establishing a landmark framework for global development partnership in which developed and developing countries agreed to take joint actions for poverty reduction. Later that same year, UN member states gathered at the World Summit on Sustainable Development in Johannesburg, South Africa, where they reaffirmed the Goals as the world's time-bound development targets.

## The means to a productive life

For the billion-plus people still living in extreme poverty, the MDGs are a life-and-death issue. Extreme poverty can be defined as "poverty that kills," depriving individuals of the means to stay alive in the face of hunger, disease, and environmental hazards. When individuals suffer from extreme poverty and lack the meager income needed even to cover basic needs, a single episode of disease, or a drought, or a pest that destroys a harvest can be the difference between life and death. In households suffering from extreme poverty, life expectancy is often around half that in the high-income world, 40 years instead of 80. It is common that of every 1,000 children born, more than 100 die before their fifth birthday, compared with fewer than 10 in the high income world. An infant born in Sub-Saharan Africa today has only a one third chance of surviving to age 65.

# Vijay Mehta

The Goals are ends in themselves, but for these households they are also capital inputs—the means to a productive life, to economic growth, and to further development. A healthier worker is a more productive worker. A better educated worker is a more productive worker. Improved water and sanitation infrastructure raises output per capita through various channels, such as reduced illness. So, many of the Goals are part of capital accumulation, defined broadly, as well as desirable objectives in their own right.

The Goals for hunger and disease are part of human capital. The Goals for water and sanitation and slum dwellers are part of infrastructure. The Goal for environmental sustainability is part of natural capital. The first Goal for income poverty is part of economic growth. And because meeting the Goals for hunger, education, gender equality, environment, and health is vital for overall economic growth and development, it is a mistake to talk simply about the rate of economic growth needed to achieve the Goals in a country. It is more helpful, particularly for the poorest countries caught in economic stagnation, to describe the range and levels of investments needed to achieve the Goals and thus to support overall economic growth.

## A linchpin to global security

The Goals not only reflect global justice and human rights—they are also vital to international and national security and stability, as emphasized by the High- Level Panel on Threats, Challenges, and Change. Poor and hungry societies are much more likely than high-income societies to fall into conflict over scarce vital resources, such as watering holes and arable land—and over scarce natural resources, such as oil, diamonds, and timber. Many world leaders in recent years have rightly stressed the powerful relationship between poverty reduction and global security. Achieving the Millennium Development Goals should therefore be placed centrally in

160

international efforts to end violent conflict, instability, and terrorism. As the High-Level Panel recommends, countries that aspire to global leadership through permanent membership on the UN Security Council have a special responsibility to promote the Goals and to fulfill international commitments to official development assistance and other kinds of support vital for achieving them. We endorse the Panel's recommended criterion of 0.7 percent of GNP in official donor assistance for developed countries aspiring to permanent membership.

Poverty increases the risks of conflict through multiple paths. Poor countries are more likely to have weak governments, making it easier for would-be rebels to grab land and vital resources. Resource scarcity can provoke population migrations and displacements that result in conflicts between social groups, as in Darfur, Sudan, in the wake of diminishing rainfall. Without productive alternatives, young people may turn to violence for material gain, or feel a sense of hopelessness, despair, and rage. Poor farmers who lack basic infrastructure and access to agricultural markets may turn in desperation to narcotics production and trade, such as growing poppy in Afghanistan or coca in the Andes. Many slums are controlled by gangs of drug traffickers and traders, who create a vicious cycle of insecurity and poverty. The lack of economically viable options other than criminal activity creates the seedbed of instability—and increases the potential for violence.

Research suggests a strong causal impact of poverty and adverse income shocks on the onset of conflict. On average a negative economic growth shock of 5 percentage points increases civil war risks by about 50 percent. And the risk of violent civil conflict declines steadily as national incomes increase. While violent conflicts surely result from a combination of factors, poverty creates conditions for igniting and sustaining conflict. The implications are twofold: investing in development is especially important to reduce the probability of conflict, and development strategies should take into consideration their possible effects on reducing the risk of conflict—or inadvertently increasing it.

**Where we stand with only a decade to go**

The world has made significant progress in achieving many of the Goals. Between 1990 and 2002 average overall incomes increased by approximately 21 percent. The number of people in extreme poverty declined by an estimated 130 million.1 Child mortality rates fell from 103 deaths per 1,000 live births a year to 88. Life expectancy rose from 63 years to nearly 65 years. An additional 8 percent of the developing world's people received access to water. And an additional 15 percent acquired access to improved sanitation services.

But progress has been far from uniform across the world—or across the Goals. There are huge disparities across and within countries. Within countries, poverty is greatest for rural areas, though urban poverty is also extensive, growing, and underreported by traditional indicators.

Sub-Saharan Africa is the epicenter of crisis, with continuing food insecurity, a rise of extreme poverty, stunningly high child and maternal mortality, and large numbers of people living in slums, and a widespread shortfall for most of the MDGs. Asia is the region with the fastest progress, but even there hundreds of millions of people remain in extreme poverty, and even fast-growing countries fail to achieve some of the nonincome Goals. Other regions have mixed records, notably Latin America, the transition economies, and the Middle East and North Africa, often with slow or no progress on some of the Goals and persistent inequalities undermining progress on others.

# Fortune Forum Code

There is also significant variation in progress toward the MDGs:

• The proportion of undernourished people is falling slowly in most regions of the world. Western Asia, Oceania, and CIS Asia are the exceptions, where the proportion has actually risen over the past decade. In Sub-Saharan Africa, some countries have seen progress, but overall proportions of undernourishment remain high with little change.

• In primary education there is progress in most regions, but Sub-Saharan Africa and South Asia are still significantly off track. Most poor children who attend primary school in the developing world learn shockingly little.

• Gender equality remains an unfulfilled goal, and the education parity target for 2005 will be missed in many countries, especially in Sub- Saharan Africa and South Asia.

• Child mortality rates have generally declined, but progress has slowed in many regions, and reversals are being recorded in the Commonwealth of Independent States. Progress has also been limited in West Asia and Oceania, and mortality remains extremely high in Sub-Saharan Africa.

• Maternal mortality remains unacceptably high in every region, reflecting low public attention to women's needs and inadequate access to sexual and reproductive health information and services, including emergency obstetric services.

• HIV/AIDS now infects about 40 million people. It is pandemic in southern Africa, and it poses a serious threat, particularly to women and adolescents, in every other developing region. The incidence of tuberculosis, still extremely high, is increasing as an opportunistic infection associated with HIV/AIDS. Malaria, an ecologically based parasite, remains a significant threat to health in many tropical regions and is pandemic in Sub-Saharan Africa.

• The share of population with access to improved drinking water supply has increased substantially. Most regions are now on track, except for Sub-Saharan Africa, Oceania, and rural areas in most regions.

• The world is not on track to meet the sanitation goal. Progress has been too slow in South Asia, Sub-Saharan Africa, and much of the rest of Asia.

• About 900 million people are estimated to live in slum-like conditions characterized by insecure tenure, inadequate housing, and a lack of access to water or sanitation. The highest share of slum dwellers is in Sub-Saharan Africa and South Asia, accounting for more than 70 percent of the urban population in many cities. Both West and East Asia (excluding China) have registered a rise in the number of slum dwellers since 1990 but a slight decline in the proportion. The same phenomenon is occurring in landlocked developing countries, small island developing states, and Least Developed Countries. In most other subregions, progress is either absent or lagging.

• All developing regions have experienced substantial environmental degradation over the past decade, which could very well worsen as a result of long-term, manmade global climate change. Many countries are struggling because their natural resource base—specifically the forests, fisheries, soil, and water that survival and livelihoods depend on—is progressively degraded and subject to rising levels of pollution. Each year, roughly 15 million hectares of forest are cleared, generally in developing countries, resulting in increases in vector-borne diseases, declines in the quantity and quality of water, and more floods, landslides, and local climate changes. The lack of good data and indicators on the environment hides the extent to which most developing regions have suffered extensive environmental degradation over the past decade and are not on track to achieving environmental sustainability.

## Why progress is so mixed

The key to achieving the Goals in low-income countries is to ensure that each person has the essential means to a productive life. In today's global economy, these means include adequate human capital, access to essential infrastructure, and core political, social, and economic rights.

In the process of economic growth, the Millennium Development Goals play two roles. First, the Goals are "ends in themselves," in that reduced hunger, improved health and education, and access to safe water and sanitation are direct goals of society. Second, the Goals are also inputs to economic growth and further development. When suitably empowered with human capital, infrastructure, and core human rights in a market-based economy, women and men can secure productive and decent employment through personal initiative. When infrastructure, health, and education are widely available, poor countries can join the global division of labor in ways that promote economic growth, raise living standards, and increase technological sophistication.

But when individuals and whole economies lack even the most basic infrastructure, health services, and education, market forces alone can accomplish little. Households and whole economies remain trapped in poverty, and fail to reap the benefits of globalization. Without basic infrastructure and human capital, countries are condemned to export a narrow range of low-margin primary commodities based on natural (physical) endowments, rather than a diversified set of exports based on technology, skills, and capital

# Vijay Mehta

investments. In such circumstances, globalization can have significant adverse effects—including brain drain, environmental degradation, biodiversity loss, capital flight, and terms-of-trade declines—rather than bring benefits through increased foreign direct investment inflows and technological advances.

Consider a typical village of subsistence farm households in a poor country, such as Afghanistan, Bhutan, Bolivia, Burkina Faso, Ethiopia, Nicaragua, or Papua New Guinea. The village lacks access to a paved road and motor transport. Also lacking electricity, its energy needs are met by extracting wood from the diminished secondary forests and woodlands. Drinking water is unsafe and latrines regularly serve as a reservoir of infection through contamination of food and the local water supply. The children are sick from diarrhea, pneumonia, and malaria.

In an African village, adults are dying of AIDS and tuberculosis, without hope of treatment. Farmers toil but do not even produce enough food to feed their families. The soils were long ago depleted of nutrients, especially nitrogen. The rains fail, and there is no backup irrigation.

In these village settings, women carry a triple burden, caring for children, the elderly, and the sick, spending long hours to gather water and fuelwood, to process and produce food, and working on farms or in family enterprises for little or no income. Impoverished families have more children than they desire because of poor access to education, contraception, decent employment opportunities, and sexual and reproductive health information and services. Education seems at best a luxury to most citizens. And since there is no emergency obstetric care, mothers die in childbirth at a hundred or more times the rate in the rich world.

Market forces alone will not rescue the village. Indeed, markets tend

166

to bypass villages with little if any monetary income, and no ready means to earn it, given the low productivity and poor connections with the regional and world economy. The village barely lives off its own food production. Without money it cannot attract doctors, teachers, or transport firms. Without electricity or access to modern fuels it cannot run food processing equipment, irrigation pumps, computers, or electric tools for carpentry or apparel. Villagers do not have enough income to save. And since infrastructure and a skilled workforce are lacking, private investors do not come. Young men and women, particularly the literate, leave the village for cities—and the best educated leave the country.

The same downward spiral applies to many urban areas. On arrival, migrants from rural areas might find employment, though informal and insecure, and they are faced with inaccessible and unaffordable housing. They take refuge in ill-serviced and overcrowded informal settlements. Many of the largest urban agglomerations in the low-income world are like extended villages, and rapidly growing cities in middle-income countries are often very poorly planned, with large areas bereft of functioning infrastructure, employment, and environmental management.

A generation or more of migrants from the countryside, combined with rapid natural population growth, results in a sprawl of densely settled humanity lacking the basics of healthcare, education, electricity, water supply, sanitation, solid waste disposal, and access to transport. People living in slums are largely excluded from enjoying their political, social, and economic rights. Some slums are so densely populated that it is not even possible to drive an ambulance into them. Diseases like tuberculosis spread like wildfire. HIV/AIDS is often rampant.

Yet practical steps can be taken to turn the tide. Both villages and cities can become part of global economic growth if they are empowered with the infrastructure and human capital to do so. If every village has a road, access to transport, a clinic, electricity, safe drinking water, education, and other essential inputs, the villagers in very poor countries will show the same determination and entrepreneurial zeal of people all over the world. If every city has a reliable electricity grid, competitive telecommunications, access to transport, accessible and affordable housing for the poor, a water and sanitation system, and access to global markets through modern ports or roads, jobs and foreign investment will flow in—rather than educated workers flowing out.

Investing in core infrastructure, human capital, and good governance therefore accomplishes several things:

• It converts subsistence farming to market-oriented farming.

• It establishes the basis for private sector–led diversified exports and economic growth.

• It enables a country to join the global division of labor in a productive way.

• It sets the stage for technological advance and eventually for an innovation-based economy.

Achieving the Goals is largely about making core investments in infrastructure and human capital that enable poor people to join the global economy, while empowering the poor with economic, political, and social rights that will enable them to make full use of infrastructure and human capital, wherever they choose to live.

**Four reasons for shortfalls in achieving the Goals**

There is no one-size-fits-all explanation for why the Goals are failing or succeeding. Each region and each Goal requires a careful analysis. We can, however, identify four overarching reasons why the Goals are not being achieved. Sometimes the problem is poor governance, marked by corruption, poor economic policy choices, and denial of human rights. Sometimes the problem is a poverty trap, with local and national economies too poor to make the needed investments. Sometimes progress is made in one part of the country but not in others, so that pockets of poverty persist. Even when overall governance is adequate, there are often areas of specific policy neglect that can have a monumental effect on their citizens' well-being. Sometimes these factors occur together, making individual problems all the more challenging to resolve.

### *Governance failures*
Economic development stalls when governments do not uphold the rule of law, pursue sound economic policy, make appropriate public investments, manage a public administration, protect basic human rights, and support civil society organizations—including those representing poor people—in national decisionmaking.

The rule of law involves security in private property and tenure rights, safety from violence and physical abuse, honesty and transparency in government functions, and predictability of government behavior according to law. Too many countries fail to achieve these basic standards, sometimes due to authoritarian rulers who use violence and corruption to hold on to power—but often because upholding the rule of law requires institutions for government accountability, and those institutions are missing.

Political and social rights should ensure equality before the law and fairness in society across groups. These rights must be substantive and not merely formal. The poor must have a meaningful say in the decisions that affect their lives. Women and girls must be assured freedom from violence and from legal, economic, and social discrimination. In many places, access to public goods and services is restricted for certain groups. Minority groups, for their language, religion, or race, suffer discrimination at the hands of more powerful groups.

Sound economic policies involve a rational balance of responsibilities between the private sector and the public sector to secure sustained and widespread economic progress. The private sector is the engine of growth in production. The public sector establishes the framework and enabling environment for growth by setting sound macroeconomic policies and providing such public goods as infrastructure, public health and education, and support for science and technology.

Public investments are crucial for a "private-based" market economy. Every successful economy relies heavily on public spending in critical areas including health, education, infrastructure (electricity grid, roads, seaports), environmental management (national parks and protected reserves, water and sanitation), information and communications, scientific research, and land for affordable housing.

Accountable and efficient public administration requires transparency and administrators who are qualified, motivated, and adequately paid. It also requires efficient management systems, to disburse and track large investments, and monitoring and evaluation systems. Many poor countries without adequate resources for decent salaries—or the checks on political abuse that provide the incentives for performance and the ability to weed out the inept and corrupt—are unable to afford an effective public sector, so they end up suffering from large-scale inefficiencies and wasted resources.

Strong civil society engagement and participation are crucial to effective governance because they bring important actors to the fore, ensure the relevance of public investments, lead to decisions that best address the people's needs as they perceive them, and serve as watchdogs for the development and implementation of government policies.

Achieving the Goals requires that all these areas of governance be properly addressed. There is no excuse for any country, no matter how poor, to abuse its citizens, deny them the equal protection of the law, or leave them victims of corruption, mismanagement, and economic irrationality. Some improvements in governance do not cost much money, if any, and some actually save money (by cutting corruption or granting land tenure, for example). Some improvements in economic outcomes are thus available at low cost, and such opportunities must not be squandered.

To achieve the Goals, governments must work actively with all constituencies, particularly civil society organizations and the private sector. Civil society organizations can help design national strategies, deliver services, defend human rights, and supervise government in the fight against corruption and misrule. And the private sector is, plainly, the place for job creation and long term income growth.

### *Poverty traps*

Many well governed countries are too poor to help themselves. Many well intentioned governments lack the fiscal resources to invest in infrastructure, social services, environmental management, and even the public administration necessary to improve governance. Further, dozens of heavily indebted poor and middle-income countries are forced by creditor governments to spend large proportions of their limited tax receipts on debt service, undermining their ability to finance vital investments in human capital and infrastructure. In a pointless and debilitating churning of resources, the creditors provide development assistance with one hand and then withdraw it in debt servicing with the other.

# Vijay Mehta

In an important recent policy initiative, the U.S. government established a set of transparent indicators that identifies poor but reasonably well governed countries that can qualify for funding from its new Millennium Challenge Account. The list of 30 countries includes Bolivia, Ghana, Mali, and Mozambique. Despite significant efforts and real progress, these countries, and many like them, pass the governance test but still fail to make adequate progress toward the Goals.

The reasons are clear. They lack the basic infrastructure, human capital, and public administration—the foundations for economic development and private sector–led growth. Without roads, soil nutrients, electricity, safe cooking fuels, clinics, schools, and adequate and affordable shelter, people are chronically hungry, burdened by disease, and unable to save. Without adequate public sector salaries and information technologies, public management is chronically weak. These countries are unable to attract private investment flows or retain their skilled workers.

The Goals create a solid framework for identifying investments that need to be made. They point to targets of public investment—water, sanitation, slum upgrading, education, health, environmental management, and basic infrastructure—that reduce income poverty and gender inequalities, improve human capital, and protect the environment. By achieving the Goals, poor countries can establish an adequate base of infrastructure and human capital that will enable them to escape from the poverty trap.

*Escaping the poverty trap.* When a country's capital stock (including physical, natural, and human capital) is too low, the economy is unproductive. Households are impoverished, and the environment is degraded. This leads to several problems:

- *Low saving rates.* Poor households use all their income to stay

172

alive, and so cannot save for the future. The few who can afford to save often have no access to formal banking.

• *Low tax revenues.* Governments lack the budgetary resources for public investments and public administrations using qualified managers and modern information systems.

• *Low foreign investment.* Foreign investors stay away from economies without basic infrastructure—those with costly and unreliable roads, ports, communication systems, and electricity.

• *Violent conflict.* Resource scarcity can often fuel latent tensions among competing groups.

• *Brain drain.* Skilled workers leave the country because of low salaries and little hope for the future.

• *Unplanned or ill-timed births and rapid population growth.* Impoverished people living in rural areas have the highest fertility rates and the largest families. Rapid population growth and shrinking farm sizes make rural poverty worse. Poor people (in rural and urban areas) have less access to information and services to space or limit their pregnancies in accord with their preferences.

• *Environmental degradation.* People in poverty lack the means to invest in the environment and the political power to limit damage to local resources, resulting in soil nutrient depletion, deforestation, overfishing, and other environmental damage. These degraded conditions undermine rural incomes, and contribute to poor health and rural-urban migration, leading to new settlement in environmentally fragile periurban areas.

All these adverse results reinforce and amplify poverty. Without private saving, public investment, and foreign investment, there is no improvement in productivity. With brain drain, population growth, environmental degradation, and ongoing risk of violence, the situation continues to degenerate.

The key to escaping the poverty trap is to raise the economy's capital stock to the point where the downward spiral ends and self-sustaining economic growth takes over. This requires a big push of basic investments between now and 2015 in public administration, human capital (nutrition, health, education), and key infrastructure (roads, electricity, ports, water and sanitation, accessible land for affordable housing, environmental management).

This process is helped by a voluntary reduction in fertility, which promotes greater investments in the health, nutrition, and education of each child. We thus strongly support programs that promote sexual and reproductive health and rights, including voluntary family planning. Critical to overall success in economic growth and poverty reduction, they can help countries meet the Goals, freeing them from the poverty trap and their dependence on aid.

*Geographical conditions make poverty traps more likely.* Some countries and regions are more vulnerable than others to falling into a poverty trap. While a history of violence or colonial rule or poor governance can leave any country bereft of basic infrastructure and human capital, physical geography plays special havoc with certain regions. Some regions need more basic infrastructure than others simply to compensate for a difficult physical environment. Here are some of the barriers that must be offset by investments:

Adverse transport conditions:
• Landlocked economies.
• Small island economies far from major markets.
• Inland populations far from coasts and navigable rivers.
• Populations living in mountains.

# Fortune Forum Code

- Long distances from major world markets.
- Very low population densities.

Adverse agroclimatic conditions:
- Low and highly variable rainfall.
- Lack of suitable conditions for irrigation.
- Nutrient-poor and nutrient-depleted soils.
- Vulnerability to pests and other postharvest losses.
- Susceptibility to the effects of climate change.

Adverse health conditions:
- High ecological vulnerability to malaria and other tropical diseases.
- High AIDS prevalence.

Other adverse conditions:
- Lack of domestic energy resources (fossil fuels, geothermal or hydropower potential).
- Small internal market and lack of regional integration.
- Vulnerability to natural hazards (tropical storms, earthquakes, volcanoes).
- Artificial borders that cut across cultural and ethnic groups.
- Proximity to countries in conflict.

Sub-Saharan Africa is especially burdened by poor geographical endowments. Africa has the highest agriculture risk (tied with South Asia), the highest transport risk, and by far the highest malaria risk. Africa is also uniquely vulnerable to drought conditions. Human vulnerability in 1980 was inversely correlated with economic growth during 1980–2000.

Africa's vulnerability is very high but not insurmountable. Indeed, our message is that geographical vulnerabilities can and need to be offset by targeted investments in infrastructure, agriculture, and health. Countries far from markets can be brought closer by adequate investments in roads and railways. Countries with nutrient-depleted soils and inadequate rainfall can be helped by special programs for soil nutrient replenishment and water management for agriculture (such as irrigation and water harvesting). Countries suffering from malaria and other endemic diseases can combat them with appropriate programs of prevention and control. Yet such investments are costly—too costly for the poorest countries to bear on their own—and so require much greater help from the donor countries.

### *Pockets of poverty*

Most economies experience considerable variation in household incomes, so even middle-income countries may have large numbers of extremely poor households, especially large countries with considerable regional and ethnic diversity. Economic development often leaves some parts of an economy, or some groups in society, far behind. This occurs both in lagging regions and in cities, where a growing proportion of the poor live in slums. In many countries there are cities within cities—a dual reality of haves and have-nots in close proximity. In many cases, geographical disadvantages (distance from markets) are worsened by the political disempowerment of minority groups.

The major policy implication for middle-income countries is to ensure that critical investments—in infrastructure, human capital, and public administration— get channeled to lagging regions, including slums, and to social groups excluded from the political process and economic benefits. Some notable lagging regions include:

• Western China, burdened by great distance from the eastern coast.
• Southern Mexico, burdened by tropical diseases, agronomic risks, great distances from the major U.S. market, and political marginalization of the indigenous peasant populations.

# Fortune Forum Code

- Northeastern Brazil, burdened by vulnerability to drought and a long history of heavily concentrated land ownership.
- The Gangetic states in India, burdened by low-productivity agriculture, long distances to coastal trade, and a large landless population.

### *Areas of specific policy neglect*
Some Goals are not being met simply because policymakers are unaware of the challenges, unaware of what to do, or neglectful of core public issues. Environmental policy is often grossly neglected because of politically weak environmental ministries, even weaker law enforcement, and considerable deficiencies in information and in the capacity to act on that information. Also common are gender biases in public investment and social and economic policies.

Throughout the developing world and even in middle-income countries, maternal mortality ratios remain appallingly high. High maternal mortality and morbidity have a specific major remedy: access to emergency obstetric care. Despite its life-saving potential, there has been a pervasive underinvestment in this service and in the health systems to deliver it. Adolescents are also widely underserved for life skills, nutrition information, education and employment opportunities, and sexual and reproductive health information and services. Investments in child and neonatal health have also been grossly insufficient. All of these areas of neglect could be addressed through strengthening the management and service delivery of district-level health systems.

Vijay Mehta
# Constitution of the World Health Organization[43]

THE STATES Parties to this Constitution declare, in conformity with the Charter of the United Nations, that the following principles are basic to the happiness, harmonious relations and security of all peoples:

Health is a state of complete physical, mental and social well-being and not merely the absence of disease or infirmity.

The enjoyment of the highest attainable standard of health is one of the fundamental rights of every human being without distinction of race, religion, political belief, economic or social condition.

The health of all peoples is fundamental to the attainment of peace and security and is dependent upon the fullest co-operation of individuals and States.

The achievement of any State in the promotion and protection of health is of value to all.

Unequal development in different countries in the promotion of health and control of disease, especially communicable disease, is a common danger.

Healthy development of the child is of basic importance; the ability to live harmoniously in a changing total environment is essential to

---

43

such development.

The extension to all peoples of the benefits of medical, psychological and related knowledge is essential to the fullest attainment of health.

Informed opinion and active co-operation on the part of the public are of the utmost importance in the improvement of the health of the people.

Governments have a responsibility for the health of their peoples which can be fulfilled only by the provision of adequate health and social measures.

ACCEPTING THESE PRINCIPLES, and for the purpose of co-operation among themselves and with others to promote and protect the health of all peoples, the Contracting Parties agree to the present Constitution and hereby establish the World Health Organization as a specialized agency within the terms of Article 57 of the Charter of the United Nations.

## CHAPTER I - OBJECTIVE

*Article 1*
The objective of the World Health Organization (hereinafter called the Organization) shall be the attainment by all peoples of the highest possible level of health.

## CHAPTER II - FUNCTIONS

*Article 2*
In order to achieve its objective, the functions of the Organization shall be:

# Vijay Mehta

*(a)* to act as the directing and co-ordinating authority on international health work;

*(b)* to establish and maintain effective collaboration with the United Nations, specialized agencies, governmental health administrations, professional groups and such other organizations as may be deemed appropriate;

*(c)* to assist Governments, upon request, in strengthening health services;

*(d)* to furnish appropriate technical assistance and, in emergencies, necessary aid upon the request or acceptance of Governments;

*(e)* to provide or assist in providing, upon the request of the United Nations, health services and facilities to special groups, such as the peoples of trust territories;

*(f)* to establish and maintain such administrative and technical services as may be required, including epidemiological and statistical services;

*(g)* to stimulate and advance work to eradicate epidemic, endemic and other diseases;

*(h)* to promote, in co-operation with other specialized agencies where necessary, the prevention of accidental injuries;

*(i)* to promote, in co-operation with other specialized agencies where necessary, the improvement of nutrition, housing, sanitation, recreation, economic or working conditions and other aspects of environmental hygiene;

# Fortune Forum Code

*(j)* to promote co-operation among scientific and professional groups which contribute to the advancement of health;

*(k)* to propose conventions, agreements and regulations, and make recommendations with respect to international health matters and to perform such duties as may be assigned thereby to the Organization and are consistent with its objective;

*(l)* to promote maternal and child health and welfare and to foster the ability to live harmoniously in a changing total environment;

*(m)* to foster activities in the field of mental health, especially those affecting the harmony of human relations;

*(n)* to promote and conduct research in the field of health;

*(o)* to promote improved standards of teaching and training in the health, medical and related professions;

*(p)* to study and report on, in co-operation with other specialized agencies where necessary, administrative and social techniques affecting public health and medical care from preventive and curative points of view, including hospital services and social security;

*(q)* to provide information, counsel and assistance in the field of health;

*(r)* to assist in developing an informed public opinion among all peoples on matters of health;

*(s)* to establish and revise as necessary international nomenclatures of diseases, of causes of death and of public health practices;

*(t)* to standardize diagnostic procedures as necessary;

*(u)* to develop, establish and promote international standards with respect to food, biological, pharmaceutical and similar products;

*(v)* generally to take all necessary action to attain the objective of the Organization.

**CHAPTER III - MEMBERSHIP AND ASSOCIATE MEMBERSHIP**

*Article 3*

Membership in the Organization shall be open to all States.

*Article 4*

Members of the United Nations may become Members of the Organization by signing or otherwise accepting this Constitution in accordance with the provisions of Chapter XIX and in accordance with their constitutional processes.

*Article 5*

The States whose Governments have been invited to send observers to the International Health Conference held in New York, 1946, may become Members by signing or otherwise accepting this Constitution in accordance with the provisions of Chapter XIX and in accordance with their constitutional processes provided that such signature or acceptance shall be completed before the first session of the Health Assembly.

*Article 6*

Subject to the conditions of any agreement between the United

# Fortune Forum Code

Nations and the Organization, approved pursuant to Chapter XVI, States which do not become Members in accordance with Articles 4 and 5 may apply to become Members and shall be admitted as Members when their application has been approved by a simple majority vote of the Health Assembly.

*Article 7* ₁

If a Member fails to meet its financial obligations to the Organization or in other exceptional circumstances, the Health Assembly may, on such conditions as it thinks proper, suspend the voting privileges and services to which a Member is entitled. The Health Assembly shall have the authority to restore such voting privileges and services.

*Article 8*

Territories or groups of territories which are not responsible for the conduct of their international relations may be admitted as Associate Members by the Health Assembly upon application made on behalf of such territory or group of territories by the Member or other authority having responsibility for their international relations. Representatives of Associate Members to the Health Assembly should be qualified by their technical competence in the field of health and should be chosen from the native population. The nature and extent of the rights and obligations of Associate Members shall be determined by the Health Assembly.

## CHAPTER IV - ORGANS

*Article 9*

The work of the Organization shall be carried out by:

*(a)* The World Health Assembly (herein called the Health Assembly);

*(b)* The Executive Board (hereinafter called the Board);

*(c)* The Secretariat.

## CHAPTER V - THE WORLD HEALTH ASSEMBLY

*Article 10*

The Health Assembly shall be composed of delegates representing Members.

*Article 11*

Each Member shall be represented by not more than three delegates, one of whom shall be designated by the Member as chief delegate. These delegates should be chosen from among persons most qualified by their technical competence in the field of health, preferably representing the national health administration of the Member.

*Article 12*

Alternates and advisers may accompany delegates.

*Article 13*

The Health Assembly shall meet in regular annual session and in such special sessions as may be necessary. Special sessions shall be convened at the request of the Board or of a majority of the Members.

# Fortune Forum Code

*Article 14*

The Health Assembly, at each annual session, shall select the country or region in which the next annual session shall be held, the Board subsequently fixing the place. The Board shall determine the place where a special session shall be held.

*Article 15*

The Board, after consultation with the Secretary-General of the United Nations, shall determine the date of each annual and special session.

*Article 16*

The Health Assembly shall elect its President and other officers at the beginning of each annual session. They shall hold office until their successors are elected.

*Article 17*
The Health Assembly shall adopt its own rules of procedure.

*Article 18*

The functions of the Health Assembly shall be:

*(a)* to determine the policies of the Organization;

*(b)* to name the Members entitled to designate a person to serve on the Board;

Vijay Mehta
# The Kyoto Protocol

*A brief summary[44]*

The Kyoto Protocol to the United Nations Framework Convention on Climate Change strengthens the international response to climate change. Adopted by consensus at the third session of the Conference of the Parties (COP3) in December 1997, it contains legally binding emissions targets for Annex I (developed) countries for the post-2000 period.

By arresting and reversing the upward trend in greenhouse gas emissions that started in these countries 150 years ago, the Protocol promises to move the international community one step closer to achieving the Convention's ultimate objective of preventing "dangerous anthropogenic [man-made] interference with the climate system".

The developed countries commit themselves to reducing their collective emissions of six key greenhouse gases by at least 5%. This group target will be achieved through cuts of 8% by Switzerland, most Central and East European states, and the European Union (the EU will meet its target by distributing different rates among its member states); 7% by the US; and 6% by Canada, Hungary, Japan, and Poland. Russia, New Zealand, and Ukraine are to stabilize their emissions, while Norway may increase emissions by up to 1%, Australia by up to 8%, and Iceland 10%. The six gases are to be combined in a "basket", with reductions in individual gases translated into "$CO_2$ equivalents" that are then added up to produce a single figure.

---

[44] http://ec.europa.eu/environment/climat/kyoto.htm. See also http://unfccc.int

# Fortune Forum Code

Each country's emissions target must be achieved by the period 2008-2012. It will be calculated as an average over the five years. "Demonstrable progress" towards meeting the target must be made by 2005. Cuts in the three most important gases – carbon dioxide ($CO_2$), methane ($CH_4$), and nitrous oxide ($N_2O$) - will be measured against a base year of 1990 (with exceptions for some countries with economies in transition).

Cuts in three long-lived industrial gases – hydrofluorocarbons (HFCs), perfluorocarbons (PFCs), and sulphur hexafluoride ($SF_6$) - can be measured against either a 1990 or 1995 baseline. (A major group of industrial gases, chlorofluorocarbons, or CFCs, are dealt with under the 1987 Montreal Protocol on Substances that Deplete the Ozone Layer.)

Actual emission reductions will be much larger than 5%. Compared with emissions levels projected for the year 2000, the richest industrialized countries (OECD members) will need to reduce their collective output by about 10%. This is because many of these countries will not succeed in meeting their earlier non-binding aim of returning emissions to 1990 levels by the year 2000; their emissions have in fact risen since 1990. While the countries with economies in transition have experienced falling emissions since 1990, this trend is now reversing.

Therefore, for the developed countries as a whole, the 5% Protocol target represents an actual cut of around 20% when compared with the emissions levels that are projected for 2010 if no emissions-control measures are adopted.

Countries will have a certain degree of flexibility in how they make and measure their emissions reductions. In particular, an international "emissions trading" regime will be established allowing industrialized countries to buy and sell emissions credits amongst themselves. They will also be able to acquire "emission reduction units" by financing certain kinds of projects in other developed countries through a mechanism known as Joint Implementation. In addition, a "Clean Development Mechanism" for promoting sustainable development will enable industrialized countries to finance emissions-reduction projects in developing countries and receive credit for doing so. The operational guidelines for these various schemes are being elaborated under a two-year Plan of Action that is to conclude at COP6.

They will pursue emissions cuts in a wide range of economic sectors. The Protocol encourages governments to cooperate with one another, improve energy efficiency, reform the energy and transportation sectors, promote renewable forms of energy, phase out inappropriate fiscal measures and market imperfections, limit methane emissions from waste management and energy systems, and protect forests and other carbon "sinks".

The measurement of changes in net emissions (calculated as emissions minus removals of $CO_2$) from forests is methodologically complex and still needs to be clarified.

The Protocol will advance the implementation of existing commitments by all countries. Under the Convention, both developed and developing countries agree to take measures to limit emissions and promote adaptation to future climate change impacts; submit information on their national climate change programmes and inventories; promote technology transfer; cooperate on scientific and technical research; and promote public awareness, education, and training. The Protocol also reiterates the need to provide "new and additional" financial resources to meet the "agreed full costs" incurred by developing countries in carrying out these commitments.

# Fortune Forum Code

The Conference of the Parties (COP) of the Convention will also serve as the meeting of the Parties (MOP) for the Protocol. This structure is expected to reduce costs and facilitate the management of the intergovernmental process. Parties to the Convention that are not Parties to the Protocol will be able to participate in Protocol-related meetings as observers.

The new agreement will be periodically reviewed. The Parties will take "appropriate action" on the basis of the best available scientific, technical, and socio-economic information. The first review will take place at the second COP session serving the Protocol. Talks on commitments for the post-2012 period must start by 2005.

The Protocol was opened for signature for one year starting 16 March 1998. It will enter into force 90 days after it has been ratified by at least 55 Parties to the Convention, including developed countries representing at least 55% of the total 1990 carbon dioxide emissions from this group. In the meantime, governments continue to carry out their commitments under the Climate Change Convention. In line with a Plan of Action agreed at the fourth COP in Buenos Aires in November 1998, they are working on many practical issues relating to the Protocol and its future implementation at their regular COP and subsidiary body meetings.

The Kyoto Protocol entered into force on 16 February 2005.

Vijay Mehta

# UNESCO Declaration On a Culture Of Peace[45]

A programme of action

The General Assembly,

Recalling the Charter of the United Nations including the purposes and principles contained therein,

Recalling the constitution of the UNESCO which states that 'since wars begin in the minds of men, it is in the minds of men that the defences of peace must be constructed',

Recalling also the Universal Declaration of Human Rights and other relevant international instruments of the United Nations system,

Recognizing that peace is not only the absence of conflict, but requires a positive, dynamic participatory process where dialogue is encouraged and conflicts are solved in a spirit of mutual understanding and cooperation,

Recognizing also that the end of the cold war has widened possibilities for strengthening a culture of peace,

Expressing deep concern about the persistence and proliferation of violence and conflict in various parts of the world,

Recognizing further the need to eliminate all forms of discrimination and intolerance, including those based on race, color, sex, language,

---

[45] http://www.unesco.org/cpp/uk/declarations/2000.htm

# Fortune Forum Code

religion, political or other opinion, national, ethnic or social origin, property, disability, birth or other status,

Recalling its resolution 52/15 proclaiming the year 2000 the 'International Year for the
Culture of Peace' and its resolution 53/25 proclaiming the period 2001-2010 as the 'International Decade for a Culture of Peace and Non-Violence for the Children of the World',

Recognizing the important role UNESCO continues to play in the promotion of a culture of peace,

1. Solemnly proclaims this *Declaration on a Culture of Peace* to the end that governments, international organizations and civil society may be guided in their activity by its provisions to promote and strengthen a culture of peace in the new millennium.

Article 1: A culture of peace is a set of values, attitudes, traditions and modes of behaviour and ways of life based on:

- Respect for life, ending of violence and promotion and practice of non-violence through education, dialogue and cooperation;
- Full respect for the principles of sovereignty, territorial integrity and political independence of States and non-intervention in matters which are essentially within the domestic jurisdiction of any State, in accordance with the Charter of the United Nations and international law;
- Full Respect for and promotion of all human rights and fundamental freedoms;
- Commitment to peaceful settlement of conflicts;
- Efforts to meet the developmental and environmental needs of present and future generations;
- Respect for and promotion of the right to development;

- Respect for and promotion of equal rights of and opportunities for women and men;
- Respect for and promotion of the rights of everyone to freedom of expression, opinion and information;
- Adherence to the principles of freedom, justice, democracy, tolerance, solidarity, cooperation, pluralism, cultural diversity, dialogue and understanding at all levels of society and among nations;

and fostered by an enabling national and international environment conducive to peace;

Article 2: Progress in the fuller development of a culture of peace comes about through values, attitudes, modes of behaviour and ways of life conducive to the promotion of peace among individuals, groups and nations;

Article 3: The fuller development of a culture of peace is integrally linked to:

- Promoting peaceful settlement of conflicts, mutual respect and understanding and international cooperation;
- Compliance with international obligations under the Charter of the United Nations and international law;
- Promoting democracy, development and universal respect for and observance of all human rights and fundamental freedoms;
- Enabling people at all levels to develop skills of dialogue, negotiation, consensus building and peaceful resolution of differences;
- Strengthening democratic institutions and ensuring full participation in the development process;
- Eradicating poverty and illiteracy and reducing inequalities within and among nations;

# Fortune Forum Code

- Promoting sustainable economic and social development;
- Eliminating all forms of discrimination against women through their empowerment and equal representation at all levels of decision-making;
- Ensuring respect for and promotion and protection of the rights of children;
- Ensuring free flow of information at all levels and enhancing access thereto;
- Increasing transparency and accountability in governance;
- Eliminate all forms of racism, racial discrimination, xenophobia and related intolerance;
- Advancing understanding, tolerance and solidarity among all civilizations, peoples and cultures, including towards ethnic, religious and linguistic minorities;
- Full realization of the rights of all peoples, including those living under colonial or other forms of alien domination or foreign occupation, to self-determination enshrined in the Charter of the United Nations and embodied in the international covenants on human rights, as well as in the Declaration on the Granting of Independence to Colonial Countries and Peoples contained in GA Resolution 1514 (XV) of 14 December 1960;

Article 4: Education at all levels is one of the principal means to build a culture of peace. In this context, human rights education is of particular importance;

Article 5: Governments have an essential role in promoting and strengthening a culture of peace;

Article 6: Civil society needs to be fully engaged in fuller development of a culture of peace;

# Vijay Mehta

Article 7: The educative and informative role of the media contributes to the promotion of a culture of peace;

Article 8: A key role in the promotion of a culture of peace belongs to parents, teachers, politicians, journalists, religious bodies and groups, intellectuals, those engaged in scientific, philosophical and creative and artistic activities, health and humanitarian workers, social workers, managers at various levels as well as to non-governmental organizations;

Article 9: The United Nations should continue to play a critical role in the promotion and strengthening of a culture of peace worldwide,

---

## B
## Programme of Action on a Culture of Peace

The General Assembly,

Bearing in mind the Declaration on a Culture of Peace adopted on 13 September 1999;

Recalling its resolution 52/15 of 20 November 1997, by which it proclaimed the year 2000 the International Year for the Culture of Peace, as well as its resolution 53/25 of 10 November 1998, by which it proclaimed the period 2001-2010 as the International Decade for a Culture of Peace and Non-violence for the Children of the World;

1. Adopts the following Programme of Action on a Culture of Peace,

A. Aims, strategies and main actors

# Fortune Forum Code

1. The Programme of Action should serve as the basis for the International Year for the Culture, of Peace and the International Decade for a Culture of Peace and Non-violence for the Children of the World.

2. Member States are encouraged to take actions for promoting a culture of peace at the national level as well as at the regional and international levels.

3. Civil society should be involved at the local, regional and national levels to widen the scope of activities on a culture of peace.

4. The United Nations system should strengthen its on-going efforts promoting a culture of peace.

5. UNESCO should continue to play its important role in and make major contributions to the promotion of a culture of peace.

6. Partnerships between and among the various actors as set out in the Declaration should be encouraged and strengthened for a global movement for a culture of peace.

7. A culture of peace could be promoted through sharing of information among actors on their initiatives in this regard.

8. Effective implementation of this Programme of Action requires mobilization of resources, including financial resources, by interested governments, organizations and individuals.

B. Strengthening actions at the national, regional and international levels by all relevant actors through:

# Vijay Mehta

9. Actions fostering a culture of peace through education:

- Reinvigorate national efforts and international cooperation to promote the goals of education for all with a view to achieving human, social and economic development and for promoting a culture of peace;
- Ensure that children, from an early age, benefit from education on the values, attitudes, modes of behaviour and ways of life to enable them to resolve any dispute peacefully and in a spirit of respect for human dignity and of tolerance and non-discrimination.
- Involve children in activities for instilling in them the values and goals of a culture of peace;
- Ensure equality of access for women, especially girls, to education;
- Encourage revision of educational curricula, including textbooks bearing in mind the 1995 Declaration and Integrated Framework of Action on Education for Peace, Human Rights and Democracy for which technical cooperation should be provided by UNESCO upon request;
- Encourage and strengthen efforts by actors as identified in the Declaration, in particular UNESCO, aimed at developing values and skills conducive to a culture of peace, including education and training in promoting dialogue and consensus-building;
- Strengthen the ongoing efforts of the relevant entities of the United Nations system aimed at training and education, where appropriate, in the areas of conflict prevention/crisis management, peaceful settlement of disputes as well as in post-conflict peace-building;
- Expand initiatives promoting a culture of peace undertaken by institutions of higher education in various parts of the world including the United Nations University, the University

# Fortune Forum Code

of Peace and the UNITWIN/UNESCO Chairs Programme;

10. Actions to promote sustainable economic and social development:

- Undertake comprehensive actions on the basis of appropriate strategies and agreed targets to eradicate poverty through national and international efforts, including through international cooperation;
- Strengthening the national capacity for implementation of policies and programmes designed to reduce economic and social inequalities within nations through, inter alia, international cooperation;
- Promoting effective and equitable development-oriented and durable solutions to the external debt and debt-servicing problems of developing countries, inter alia, through debt relief;
- Reinforcement of actions at all levels to implement national strategies for sustainable food security including the development of actions to mobilize and optimize the allocation and utilization of resources from all sources, including through international cooperation such as resources coming from debt relief;
- Further efforts to ensure that development process is participatory and that development projects involve the full participation of all;
- Integrating a gender perspective and empowering women and girls should be an integral part of the development process;
- Development strategies should include special measures focusing on needs of women and children as well as groups with special needs;
- Development assistance in post-conflict situations should strengthen rehabilitation, reintegration and reconciliation processes involving all engaged in the conflict;

- Capacity-building in development strategies and projects to ensure environmental sustainability, including preservation and regeneration of the natural resource base;
- Removing obstacles to the realization of the right of peoples to self-determination, in particular of peoples living under colonial or other forms alien domination or foreign occupation, which adversely affect their social and economic development;

11. Actions to promote respect for all human rights:

- Full implementation of the Vienna Declaration and Programme of Action;
- Encouraging development of national plans of action for the promotion and protection of all human rights;
- Strengthening of national institutions and capacities in the field of human rights, including through national human rights institutions;
- Realization and implementation of the right to development, as established in the Declaration on the Right to Development and the Vienna Declaration and Programme of Action;
- Achievement of the goals of the United Nations Decade for Human Rights Education (1995-2004);
- Disseminate and promote the Universal Declaration of Human Rights at all levels;
- Further support to the activities of the United Nations High Commissioner for Human Rights in the fulfillment of her/his mandate as established in UNGA resolution 48/141 as well as the responsibilities set by subsequent resolutions and decisions;

12. Actions to ensure equality between women and men:

- Integration of a gender perspective into the implementation of all relevant international instruments;
- Further implementation of international instruments promoting equality between women and men;
- Implementation of the Beijing Platform for Action with adequate resources and political will, and through, inter alia, the elaboration, implementation and follow-up of the national plans of action;
- Promote equality between women and men in economic, social and political decision making;
- Further strengthening of efforts by the relevant entities of the United Nations system for the elimination of all forms of discrimination and violence against women;
- Provision of support and assistance to women who have become victims of any forms of violence, including in the home, workplace and during armed conflicts;

13. Actions to foster democratic participation:

- Reinforcement of the full range of actions to promote democratic principles and practices;
- Special emphasis on democratic principles and practices at all levels of formal, informal and non-formal education;
- Establishment and strengthening of national institutions and processes that promote and sustain democracy through, inter alia, training and capacity-building of public officials;
- Strengthening democratic participation through, inter alia, the provision of electoral assistance upon the request of States concerned and based on relevant United Nations guidelines;
- Combat terrorism, organized crime, corruption as well as production, trafficking and consumption of illicit drugs and money laundering as they undermine democracies and impede the fuller development of a culture of peace;

# Vijay Mehta

14. Actions to advance understanding, tolerance and solidarity:

- Implementation of the Declaration of Principles of Tolerance and Follow-up Plan of Action for the United Nations Year of Tolerance (1995);
- Support activities in the context of the United Nations International Year of Dialogue among Civilizations in the year 2001;
- Study further the local or indigenous practices and traditions of dispute settlement and promotion of tolerance with the objective of learning from those;
- Support actions that foster understanding, tolerance and solidarity throughout society, in particular with vulnerable groups;
- Further supporting the attainment of the goals of the International Decade of the World's Indigenous People;
- Support actions that foster tolerance and solidarity with refugees and displaced persons bearing in mind the objective of facilitating their voluntary return and social integration;
- Support actions that foster tolerance and solidarity with migrants;
- Promotion of increased understanding, tolerance and cooperation among all peoples, inter alia, through appropriate use of new technologies and dissemination of information;
- Support actions that foster understanding, tolerance, solidarity and cooperation among peoples and within and among nations;

15. Actions to support participatory communication and the free flow of information and knowledge:

- Support the important role of the media in the promotion of a culture of peace;

# Fortune Forum Code

- Ensure freedom of the press and freedom of information and communication;
- Making effective use of the media for advocacy and dissemination of information on a culture of peace involving, as appropriate, the United Nations and relevant regional, national and local mechanisms;
- Promoting mass communication that enable communities to express their needs and participate in decision-making;
- Taking measures to address the issue of violence in the media including new communication technologies, inter alia, the internet;
- Increased efforts to promote the sharing of information on new information technologies, including the internet.

16. Actions to promote international peace and security:

- Promote general and complete disarmament under strict and effective international control taking into account the priorities established by the United Nations in the field of disarmament;
- Draw on, where appropriate, lessons conducive to a culture of peace learned from "military conversion" efforts as evidenced in some countries of the world;
- Emphasize the inadmissibility of acquisition of territory by war and the need to work for a just and lasting peace in all parts of the world;
- Encourage confidence building measures and efforts for negotiating peaceful settlements;
- Take measures to eliminate illicit production and traffic of small arms and light weapons;
- Support for initiatives, at the national, regional and international levels, to address concrete problems arising from post conflict situations, such as demobilization, reintegration of former combatants into society as well as

refugees and displaced persons, weapon collection programmes, exchange of information and confidence building;

- Discourage the adoption of and refrain from any unilateral measure, not in accordance with international law and the Charter of the United Nations, that impedes the full achievement of economic and social development by the population of the affected countries, in particular women and children, that hinders their well-being that creates obstacles to the full enjoyment of their human rights, including the right of everyone to a standard of living adequate for their health and well-being and their right to food, medical care and the necessary social services, while reaffirming food and medicine must not be used as a tool for political pressure;

- Refrain from military, political, economic or any other form of coercion, not in accordance with international law and the Charter of the United Nations. aimed against political independence or territorial integrity of any state;

- Recommends to give proper consideration to the issue of humanitarian impact of sanctions, in particular on women and children, with a view of minimizing humanitarian effects of sanctions;

- Promoting greater involvement of women in prevention and resolution of conflicts and in particular, in activities promoting a culture of peace in post-conflict situations;

- Promote initiatives in conflict situation such as days of tranquility to carry out immunization and medicines distribution campaigns; corridors of peace to ensure delivery of humanitarian supplies and sanctuaries of peace to respect the central role of health and medical institutions such as hospitals and clinics;

- Encourage training in techniques for the understanding, prevention and resolution of conflict for the concerned staff

# Fortune Forum Code

of the United Nations, relevant regional organizations and
Member States, upon request, where appropriate.

Vijay Mehta

# Further Reading

Amnesty International and Oxfam International, Shattered Lives: The case for tough international arms control (London, 2003).
*http://www.oxfam.org.uk/what_we_do/issues/conflict_disasters/shattered_lives.htm*

Colin Archer (2006), *Warfare or Welfare? Disarmament for Development in the 21st Century.* Geneva: International Peace Bureau.

Sabina Alkire, and Edmund Newell (2005), *What Can One Person Do?* London: Darton, Longman and Todd Ltd.

Geraldine Bedell (2005), *Make Poverty History, How You Can Help Defeat World Poverty in Seven Easy Steps.* London: Penguin Books.

Deepak Chopra (2005), *Peace Is the Way.* New York: Harmony Books.

Collier and Hoeffler (2004), The Challenge of Reducing the Global Incidence of Civil War.
*http://www.copenhagenconsensus.com/Files/Filer/CC/Papers/Conflicts_230404.pdf*

Angela Drakulich, (ed). *Global Agenda, issues before the 59th General Assembly of the United Nations.* New York: United Nations Association, USA, Inc., 2004

Lomborg, Bjorn (ed) *Global Crises, Global Solutions* (Cambridge University Press, Cambridge, 2004)

# Vijay Mehta

Louis Emmerij, Richard Jolly, and Thomas G. Weiss (2001), *Ahead of the Curve? UN Ideas and Global Challenges.* Bloomington: Indiana University Press.

ILO (2001) "An ILO Code of Practice and HIV/AIDS and the world of work." Geneva: International Labour Office.

Paul Kennedy, Dirk Messner and Franz Nuscheler (2002). *Global Trends and Global Governance.* London: Pluto Press.

John Madeley (2005), *Hungry for Trade.* London/ New York: Zed Books.

Federico Mayor and Jerome Binde, (2001), *The World Ahead: Our future in the making.* London/New York: Zed Books.

Robin Marris (1999), *Ending Poverty.* Thames & Hudson.

Vijay Mehta (2003), *Arms No More,* London: Arms Reduction Coalition.

Vijay Mehta (2005), *The United Nations and its Future in the 21$^{st}$ Century,* Nottingham: Spokesman.

N. Middleton, P. O'Keefe and R. Visser (2001), *Negotiating Poverty,* Virginia: Pluto Press

J.F. Rischard (2002), *High Noon: 20 Global Problems, 20 Years to Solve Them,* New York: Basic Books.

J. Sachs (2005), *The End of Poverty: How can we make it happen in our Lifetime,* New York: Penguin Books.

A. Sen (2001), *Development as Freedom,* Oxford University Press

# Fortune Forum Code

United Nations (2004), "A More Secure World: Our Shared Responsibility." Report of the Secretary General's High-Level Panel on Threats, Challenges and Change. New York.
http://www.un.org/secureworld/

United Nations (2005), "In Larger Freedom: Towards Security, Development and Human Rights for All." New York.
http://www.un.org/largerfreedom/

UNDP (2005), "Investing in Development: A Practical Plan to Achieve the Millennium Development Goals." New York: Earthscan.
http://www.unmillenniumproject.org/

UNDP (2002), "Human Development Report 2002." New York: Oxford University Press
http://hdr.undp.org/reports/global/2002/en/

UNDP (2005), *Coming to Grips with Malaria in the New Millennium,* New York: Earthscan.

UNDP (2005), *Environment and Human Well-being: A Practical Strategy,* New York: Earthscan.

UN-HABITAT (2006), *The State of the World's Cities: The Millennium Goals and Urban Sustainability,* New York: Earthscan.

Michael Woodin and Caroline Lucas (2004), *Green Alternatives to Globalisation A Manifesto.* London: Pluto Press.

# Useful Websites

---

**African Renaissance** http://www.african-renaissance.com

**Alliance for New Humanity** http://www.anhglobal.org

**Arms Reduction Coalition** http://www.arcuk.org

**British Overseas NGOs for Development** http://www.bond.org.uk

**British Red Cross** http://www.redcross.org.uk

**Campaign for Nuclear Disarmament** http://www.cnduk.org

**Carbon Dioxide Information Analysis Centre**
http://cdiac.esd.ornl.gov/home.html

**Carnegie Council** http://www.cceia.org

**CAFOD** http://www.cafod.org.uk

**Chatham House** - http://www.riia.org

**Clinton Global Initiative** http://www.clintonglobalinitiative.org

**Commission for Africa** http://www.commissionforafrica.org

**Concern Worldwide** http://www.concern.net

**Convention on Biological Diversity** http://www.biodiv.org

# Fortune Forum Code

**The Ecologist** http://www.theecologist.org

**The Economist Intelligence Unit**
http://www.economist.com/countries

**Fortune Forum** www.fortuneforum.org

**Friends of the Earth** http://www.foe.org

**G8** http://en.g8russia.ru

**Greenpeace** http://www.greenpeace.org

**Hague Appeal for Peace** www.haguepeace.org

**Heidelberg Institute on International Conflict Research**
http://www.hiik.de/en/index_e.htm

**The International Monetary Fund** http://www.imf.org

**International Peace Bureau** www.ipb.org

**Jubilee Debt Campaign** http://www.jubileedebtcampaign.org.uk

**London School of Economics** http://www.lse.ac.uk

**Make Poverty History** http://www.makepovertyhistory.org

**Massachusetts Institute of Technology** http://web.mit.edu

**National Centre for Public Policy Research**
http://www.nationalcenter.org

**Nature Magazine** http://www.nature.com

**OXFAM** http://www.oxfam.co.uk

**Principle Voices** http://www.principalvoices.com

**Stop Climate Chaos** http://www.stopclimatechaos.org

**TERI School of Advanced Studies** http://www.terischool.ac.in

**United Nations Organization** www.un.org

**United Nations Association** http://www.una.org.uk

**United Nations Children's Fund** http://www.unicef.org/index.php

**United Nations Declaration on a Culture of Peace**
http://www.unesco.org/cpp/uk/declarations/2000.htm

**United Nations Department for Disarmament Affairs**
http://disarmament.un.org

**United Nations Development Programme (UNDP)**
http://www.undp.org

**United Nations Environment Programme** http://www.unep.org

**United Nations Food and Agricultural Organisation**
http://www.fao.org

**United Nations International Poverty Centre** http://www.undp-povertycentre.org

**UN Office of the Secretary-General for Children and Armed Conflict**

# Fortune Forum Code

http://www.un.org/special-rep/children-armed-conflict

**Universal Declaration of Human Rights**
www.unhchr.ch/udhr.index.htm

**VM Centre for Peace** www.vmpeace.org

**Water Aid** http://www.wateraid.org/uk

**World Bank** http://www.worldbank.org

**World Disarmament Campaign** http://www.world-disarm.org.uk

**World Economic Forum** http://www.weforum.org

**World Health Organization** http://www.who.int/en

**World Wildlife Federation** www.wwf.org.uk/

# About VM Centre for Peace

---

Its main aims are:

- Working for the maintenance of durable peace and security through holistic disarmament. Finding non-violent ways of resolving armed conflicts through dialogue and global education.
- Respect for ethics, human rights and fundamental freedoms by observing accountable, transparent, democratic principles and the rule of law.
- Reforming and strengthening United Nations and its organs by adhering to international law and multilateral treaties. Promoting democracy and good governance.
- To address the challenges of globalisation, poverty, and sustainable development by implementing the Millennium Development Goals by 2015.

The objectives of the Centre are:

- To inform and promote a better understanding
- To provide a forum and disseminate policy recommendations
- To propose solutions and act on initiatives
- To be a catalyst for change by promoting public participation, debate and solutions, on critical peace, economic, environmental, social and foreign policy issues.

www.vmpeace.org

# INDEX

# INDEX

214

# INDEX

# INDEX

216